"It's not often that a street-level veteran of nitty-gritty urban ministry is also a gifted writer with an engaging style and real spiritual insight . . . but that's the rare combination you'll discover in Bruce Main. This book will do you good, and it will get you doing good."

BRIAN MCLAREN, author/speaker/activist
brianmclaren.net

"Bruce Main writes brilliantly, thinks profoundly, and daringly challenges the security that keeps us from grappling with truths about injustice and oppression. His book gets two thumbs up!"

TONY CAMPOLO, professor emeritus
Eastern University

"The Christian life is, as we have been told so many times in recent years, 'a faith journey.' But Bruce Main makes the case—with much insight and wisdom—that if we want to walk the road with Jesus, we need to follow him when he insists that we join him in crossing the road. If we do so, we'll experience people and things we would have otherwise missed along the way."

RICHARD J. MOUW, president and professor of
Christian philosophy
Fuller Theological Seminary

"If you want to experience a Christian life that makes a difference, this is the book for you. *Why Jesus Crossed the Road* calls the reader to celebrate Christian living because Jesus, our model, wants us to cross the roads he did. Be a world changer . . . cross the road."

JON R. WALLACE, president
Azusa Pacific University

"Great stories, solid theology—a probing challenge to live more like Jesus."

RONALD J. SIDER, president
Evangelicals for Social Action

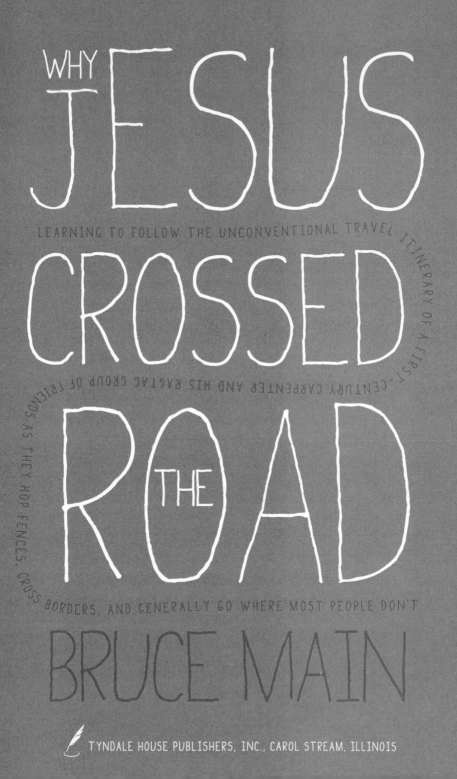

WHY JESUS CROSSED THE ROAD

LEARNING TO FOLLOW THE UNCONVENTIONAL TRAVEL ITINERARY OF A FIRST-CENTURY CARPENTER AND HIS RAGTAG GROUP OF FRIENDS AS THEY HOP FENCES, CROSS BORDERS, AND GENERALLY GO WHERE MOST PEOPLE DON'T

BRUCE MAIN

TYNDALE HOUSE PUBLISHERS, INC., CAROL STREAM, ILLINOIS

Library of Congress Cataloging-in-Publication Data

Main, Bruce.
    Why Jesus crossed the road : learning to follow the unconventional travel itinerary of a first-century carpenter and his ragtag group of friends as they hop fences, cross borders, and generally go where most people don't / Bruce Main.
        p. cm.
    Includes bibliographical references.
    ISBN 978-1-4143-2660-3 (sc)
    1. Jesus Christ—Example. 2. Travel—Religious aspects—Christianity. 3. Christian life. I. Title.
    BT304.2.M33 2010
    248.4—dc22   2009038328

To the children of Camden
With open arms, you lovingly crossed the road to me.

CONTENTS

Acknowledgments   ix
Introduction: Open the Eyes of My Heart   xi

PART ONE: WHY JESUS CROSSED THE ROAD

Chapter One: Where Did Jesus Travel?   3
Chapter Two: Welcoming Disorienting Dilemmas   11
Chapter Three: Can a Rock Really Change?   19

PART TWO: JESUS' TRAVEL ITINERARY

Chapter Four: Crossing the Road to the Poor   35
Chapter Five: Crossing the Road of Race   45
Chapter Six: Crossing the Road of Spiritual
                   Exclusivity   61
Chapter Seven: Crossing the Road to Our Enemies   79
Chapter Eight: Crossing the Road of Cultural
                   Worldview   95

PART THREE: ROADBLOCKS TO ROAD CROSSINGS

Chapter Nine: The Roadblock of Fear   109
Chapter Ten: The Roadblock of Indifference   121
Chapter Eleven: The Roadblock of Misguided
                   Theology   131

PART FOUR: THE IMPACT OF ROAD CROSSINGS

Chapter Twelve: Second-Floor Christianity and
                    the Art of Embrace   143
Chapter Thirteen: Road-Crossing Adventures:
                    A Businessman, a Pastor, a Lawyer,
                    and a Veterinarian   155

Conclusion: The Heart of the Travel Itinerary   171

Discussion Questions for Your Journey   181

Appendix A: Opportunities to Cross the Road   189
Appendix B: Elaborating on a Love Story in
                    Four Acts   191

Notes   197

About the Author   201

ACKNOWLEDGMENTS

To those who make road crossing a spiritual discipline—you provide a real glimpse of the Jesus life.

To the staff, youth, and volunteers of UrbanPromise—you admirably create a place for road crossing to occur.

To my friend and editor, Paul Keating—thanks for never wearying of improving what I send you.

To John and Donna—for providing a wonderful place to conceive this book.

To my wife, Pamela, and children, Calvin, Erin, and Madeline—for providing so many incredible moments.

Thank you.

OPEN THE EYES OF MY HEART

Loving God, we admit to attitudes that exclude rather than embrace. We prefer to associate with others who think and act as we do. . . . Awaken us to the limits of our understanding and the narrowness of our dealings.

PRESBYTERIAN PRAYER OF CONFESSION

Jim was tall, angular, and masculine—almost movie-star handsome—a warm, easily likable person who never backed down from a challenge; he was a doer in his church, planning the ski trip or the summer pool party for the young people. Jim was high octane, a roll-up-your-sleeves kind of guy who liked to get his hands dirty; when Hurricane Katrina devastated the southern coast, Jim recruited his buddies and got them to spend their vacation days stripping moldy Sheetrock from the devastated houses and repairing roofs in ninety-degree, suffocating heat; then he led service-oriented trips for youth to Mexico, Kentucky, and Maine—building homes, clearing trails.

Yet leading a mission group to Camden, New Jersey—that dread-of-a-broken-city just ten minutes (but light-years) from his home—well, that was a different matter.

Jim was telling his story to the teenagers from his church who crowded the room at UrbanPromise.[1] "When the chairman of our church's mission committee—you know what they're like— asked me to lead an exploratory trip to Camden, I was a little defensive. No, I was a lot more than *a little*." Jim was pacing back and forth, beginning to perspire as he passionately tried to let us all know his deepest feelings.

He paused. The room of teens was transfixed as Jim continued his confession. "After all, Camden is known by everybody as the *badlands*. All the local magazines and newspapers call Camden 'America's most dangerous city.' Most of us intentionally avoid it. The main freeway that divides Camden from the surrounding communities might as well be the Berlin Wall. Few people would question my apprehension to go there; most would cheer me on and call me sensible and wise and heroic. I mean, I just dug in my heels," he said, not disguising the emotion he felt. "No way! My heart was closed. I wasn't about to go to Camden."

The kids in Jim's youth group were transfixed by his openness. Mr. Positive Leader had let down his guard.

"But then, at the urgent (verging on the passionate) request of our mission director," he continued, "I reluctantly, *very* reluctantly, went down to Camden for a visit. All the time I was thinking, *This is a waste of time,* since I had already made up my mind.

"Then I met Diamond. (God uses sneaky ways to get our attention sometimes.) Diamond was a charming, beautiful little girl—around eight years old. She gently took my hand and began to lead me around her school, showing me all the classrooms, rambling on about . . . well, about everything. I was smitten."

Jim looked at the crowd. "My heart melted. She was an unassuming, intuitive little girl who never let on that she sensed my contempt. Instead, she reached out to me with love."

He brushed away a tear.

"A few minutes ago when we sang the words 'Open the eyes of my heart, Lord,' I was reminded of what happened in my life. The eyes of my heart had been shut tight toward Camden before I arrived. But then, my eyes were opened. I encourage each person here to make that your prayer—allow God the opportunity to open the eyes of your heart."

I was intrigued by what Jim said.

Actually, I'm always intrigued with *how people change*—how our attitudes change, how our perceptions change, how our hearts and minds change. Scripture describes significant changes with such phrases as "he is a new creation" (2 Corinthians 5:17) and "you have taken off your old self" (Colossians 3:9). We even sing songs about putting on the mind of Christ or exemplifying the heart of Christ in our daily actions, but at the end of the day we hold on to the same fears, prejudices, and stereotypes that we have always held. The truth is that changing—no matter how big or small a change we need to or choose to make—is a difficult process.

ROAD MARKER

Sometimes we have to cross the road to discover
the thing that will change us.

In Jim's situation, change came because he went to a place he didn't want to and encountered people he would have rather avoided. Real change wasn't because of intensified personal prayer, a voracious consumption of Scripture, or even a warm, fuzzy experience with other believers. Jim's willingness, albeit reluctant, to venture into a place he had excluded from his life dramatically changed his perception and attitude toward a place and people. And his changed perception was now changing the perception of others.

Jim's heart changed because he crossed a road, entering a place he had previously turned his back on. God's Spirit seized that moment and sparked what would become a radical change.

Roads are definitely passageways, but they can also be barriers and borders that govern our decisions, direct our movements, and control our lives. In New Jersey, where I live, roads often isolate certain communities from others. Highways don't simply get you from point A to point B. These six-lane rivers of concrete are the new "railroad tracks" that divide who is on the "right side" from who is on the "wrong side." Some borders are geographical, others are social, many are psychological. If we are completely honest, all of us have places, situations, and people that we do our best to avoid. Given a choice between taking a left turn toward that which makes us uncomfortable or a right turn toward the familiar, we take the right turn every time. Our fear may be precipitated by too much information from past negative experiences or ignorance from a lack of information. Needless to say, crossing roads and borders is tough work; it takes energy, intention, and a whole lot of courage.

As difficult as it is, it is critical to cross these roads for two reasons: First, Jesus, who models a road-crossing lifestyle, calls those who follow him to do the same. Throughout his ministry, at every turn it seemed Jesus crossed *barriers, borders*, and *boundaries*. Because of his commitment, Jesus' spiritual life was comprised of a faith that faced the realities of daily life head-on. In the travels of Jesus we find the clues to what it means to be a person committed to growing as a child of God, a person who reflects the heart and nature of God in the world. Second, in some mysterious way, God uses our road crossings to change both our lives and often the lives of those we meet along the way.

ROAD MARKER

Jesus crossed the road to model a new kind of
spiritual journey.

This book is about discovering why it is critical for Christians to view road crossing as an essential spiritual discipline. But it's not just to take in the view. By examining the life of Jesus and the lives of those who have chosen to reach across barriers and boundaries, the hope is that we can find the courage and inspiration to go and do likewise.

Bruce Main

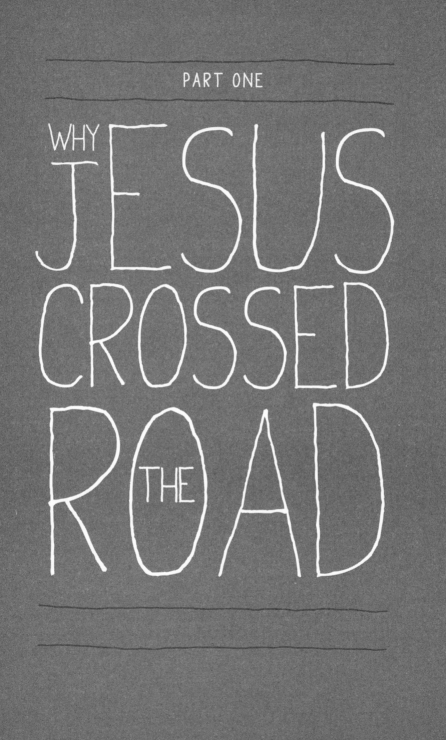

PART ONE

WHY JESUS CROSSED THE ROAD

CHAPTER ONE

WHERE DID JESUS TRAVEL?

*In this regard it is significant how Jesus routinely
crossed borders that others imagined impenetrable.*

RODNEY CLAPP[1]

"Those potholes were the size of Volkswagen Bugs," exclaimed
Frank, his arms held wide as if describing the fish that got away.
He was recounting his recent, on-purpose detour through the
north side of our city's most deteriorated neighborhood. He
wanted to make it clear that he had not made a wrong turn but
had intentionally driven through this community that would
never be mentioned as a must-see attraction.

"My wife and I always take a different route whenever we're
going home from an event," he continued with more than a hint
of sadness in his voice as he remembered that evening. "I always
try to get a different perspective wherever I go, but *your* town was
a bewildering and grim eye-opener." He paused for a moment,
reflecting. "Do you *really* believe those neighborhoods can be
improved?"

I admired Frank. He could have taken several expressways and
been home in minutes; most people do. Instead, he chose to
take out-of-the-way side streets. He drove where most people are
afraid to drive, and because of it his perspective changed.

Now he was asking me questions, seeking answers. Trying to
come to grips with the harsh realities of the inner city, he was
genuinely concerned.

Frank explained that he made it a practice to break his routines and travel new roads, and his musings underscored his curiosity. Most of us, on the other hand, choose expedience over adventure, four-lane highways over potholed side streets, the familiar over the unknown. We forget that the places we visit—or choose not to visit—profoundly affect what we see, what we hear, and what we think. But Frank altered his travel plans so that the experiences would challenge him to see life in a different way. Unbeknownst to himself, Frank was modeling a critical biblical truth, the truth so vividly demonstrated by Jesus.

WHERE DID JESUS GO?

If we read the Gospel narratives as merely a travel itinerary, what would it reveal about Jesus and his disciples? Sit down and map out the journey of Jesus during his three years of public ministry. What do his stops say about his interests, concerns, faith, mission, commitments, and purposes?

I think it's relevant and interesting that Jesus initiated his public ministry in Capernaum—a poor fishing village, not a bustling metropolis. He spent time in graveyards, traveled through Samaria, went to ethnically mixed cities like Tyre and Sidon, and intentionally returned to a hostile Jerusalem. These places were not simply locations, without significant meaning or repercussions. Each of his destinations and interactions with various people groups represented something for Jesus; and where he went and what transpired there provide us with a deeper glimpse into his mission and purpose on earth. In the end, the fullness of Jesus' life cannot be interpreted only on the basis of what he taught. His actions also speak to us across the centuries . . . sometimes even louder than his words.

We all know that the places we visit provide insight into our interests and life purposes—for example, a trip to the Acropolis reveals an interest in ancient Greek culture; a week spent in Yosemite National Park shows a love of nature and the outdoors.

A weekend in Las Vegas, well, that at least suggests a curiosity about gambling and partying. (Of course, you could be an insomniac and need a good restaurant at three in the morning. Las Vegas never sleeps.)

The people and places we visit reveal more about our commitments and convictions than what we espouse with our lips. Our travel plans make a moral and spiritual statement; they reveal how we spend our most sacred gifts—time, energy, and resources. They also reveal an attitude of the heart.

ROAD MARKER

Jesus crossed the road to let his actions speak
louder than his words.

The same is true of Jesus: he chose how he spent his time. I resist the temptation to believe that he was divinely programmed—having no choice where he would stop for lunch, take a nap, or bunk down at the end of each day. God did not insert a fresh computer chip in Jesus' brain that outlined the next day's activities and encounters. Jesus made choices.

But even if we argue that Jesus was divinely programmed, we would have to admit that his travel schedule displayed the consistent and varied interests of God. The places where Jesus spent his time provide important insights into the heart and will of God.

For example, if Jesus spent all his time with the upper crust of society, it would speak volumes about God's potential bias toward the rich and powerful. If, like some mystic, Jesus spent all his time in a far-off desert cave, it would provide deeper insight into the meaning of a holy life. But Jesus did neither exclusively. Yes, he spent time with wealthy people, even going to their parties, and he did spend time in isolation. But in most of his public life Jesus was engaged with people who lived in small towns, capital cities, villages, wherever—each person representing the diversity of the human family in all aspects of his or her life.

A closer examination reveals that Jesus even traveled to places that one might not associate with a holy man or an itinerate preacher; instead he crossed roads and barriers that other people were afraid to cross. Metaphorically speaking, Jesus crossed the "roads" that divided people on the basis of race, ethnicity, religious beliefs, and economic standing. Jesus' road-crossing actions demonstrated that he did not follow the religious and societal protocols of his day. In a world that was governed strictly by geographical, religious, and social barriers, Jesus was audacious enough to cross the roads that kept people in safe categories. And by crossing those roads Jesus demonstrated that a God-following life is a life of inclusion and expansion—not an exclusive and limited life that avoids certain kinds of people and certain places. The God-following life for Jesus was a life committed to entering the lives and stories of all kinds of people. It was a life that challenged barriers.

Rodney Clapp puts it powerfully when he writes,

He welcomed children and talked publicly to women. He ate with tax collectors. He stepped inside the borders of the stoning circle and stood on the side of the adulteress. He touched the sick and the leprous. And of course he famously suggested that purity was not a matter of what comes from the outside in, but of what comes from the inside out. He treated borders as . . . "places of encounter" as permeable and alive as the skin that covers our bodies.[2]

At the heart of Jesus' public ministry was his willingness to convert barriers into bridges—bridges where differences could be united and embraced.

THE LOST DISCIPLINE

If I asked one hundred Christians how I could or should grow in my faith, I guarantee that I would hear the following: attend church regularly, get involved in a small group, read the Bible, pray daily, and avoid the temptation of sin. Some believers would mention the need for fasting; others might insist that meditation is primary. When most of us think of spiritual growth and personal transformation, we tend to think of more traditional disciplines. No one would claim road crossing as an essential spiritual discipline.

But here's the problem. I believe that we can faithfully read the Bible, pray, fast . . . and never really change. We can go to church all our lives and still hold bigoted views of others, live in fear, and never develop the capacity to see beyond our own kind of people. Church history is full of such examples. Christians sat in church Sunday after Sunday for years, well aware of the atrocities happening to their African American brothers and sisters, and still resisted granting them their basic civil rights. Some high-profile Christian leaders, who have spent a lifetime studying the Scriptures, still make comments that reveal a complete ignorance of other cultures and values. Despite centuries of faithful Christian service and enormous contributions, women can still be marginalized by pious, chauvinistic, Bible-believing men. Dedicated, lifelong church elders can make it uncomfortable for outsiders to feel welcome and can wield power in unbelievably childish ways. A life dedicated to the practice of traditional spiritual disciplines does not guarantee growth toward full Christian maturity.

The problem with the traditional spiritual disciplines is that they can all be done in isolation—both privately and within groups—and simply reinforce what we want to believe. The problem with a spiritual life being exercised in isolation is that it allows people to grow without the perspective of others.

Surrounding ourselves with people who think, act, look, and even smell like us usually leads toward a distorted growth pattern or no growth at all. We may ultimately experience a small fraction of what God wants for our lives, even with erroneous views going unchallenged. But ultimately our growth becomes biased, unbalanced, and stunted.

This is why the discipline of road crossing is so critical to add to our list of spiritual disciplines.

ROAD MARKER

Sometimes we have to cross the road to find
Jesus' footprints ahead of us on the path.

Some people might argue that crossing roads—going to those places we find uncomfortable and out of the way—should be the end result of our interior development. To put it another way, we engage in spiritual disciplines to prepare ourselves to reach out to other people. Crossing roads, you might argue, should be placed in the category of "Christian service" or "social action," not spiritual discipline.

I would argue differently. Jesus did not have a "spiritual life" with a little service tacked on. Nor did he have an occasional service project with a few hours of spiritual disciplines scheduled in his downtime. Rather, there is an integration of these two realities expressed in the life of Jesus. Action and contemplation interact with one another in dynamic relationship. They feed each other. They shape each other. For Jesus, every aspect of life had the potential of deepening his relationship with God and expanding his notion of what it meant to live as God's child.

From Jesus we learn that the act of road crossing—crossing barriers—places us in conflicted situations that challenge our narrow vision of spiritual growth. Conflict can be healthy and lead to growth: it can call us to reevaluate our lives, our commitments, our perspectives, our prejudices, and our vision for God's work in the world.

Since the Scriptures claim that Jesus "grew in wisdom and stature" (Luke 2:52) we must look to his life as a model for our own growth. And since Jesus spent a good deal of his time crossing barriers erected by his society and its religious leaders, we must understand the nature of his crossings and follow his lead.

CHAPTER TWO

WELCOMING DISORIENTING DILEMMAS

*What gives value to travel is fear. It is the fact that, at
a certain moment, when we are so far from our own
country we are seized by a vague fear, and an instinc-
tive desire to go back to the protection of old habits.
This is the most obvious benefit of travel. At that
moment we are feverish but also porous.*

ALBERT CAMUS[1]

My spiritual life changed the first time I walked into a housing
project in southwest Philadelphia. As an English major in my
junior year at a Southern California Christian college, I was very
comfortable in my protective bubble. On a whim one summer
I signed up for eight weeks of mission work on the East Coast.
I had done a little evangelistic outreach in high school and spent
time in Los Angeles. But I had no idea what living in the midst
of urban poverty would be like, even though kind people tried to
warn me. I was twenty-two, was about to cross a very wide road,
and had no clue. Not only would I cross the country, I would
cross the road of race and class, and take up residence in a notorious inner-city community.

Although I had no way to process the experience then, I was having what developmental theorists call a "disorienting dilemma."
Everything normative in my life had been turned upside down.
I didn't have the security of being in the majority. I was pretty
much the only white college kid in the community other than a

few others on the team. I had no social props to give me comfort or direction, no sense of security, nothing. The affirmations of the "have-a-great-summer" friends were replaced by my vulnerability. As French existentialist Albert Camus described, I was "feverish but also porous." In my words, I was a semiarticulate, knee-knocking college student whose stomach was in knots all the time.

Unfortunately, my Psychology 101 class back on the other side of the continent had not exposed me to the work of the developmental theorist Jack Mezirow. His insights might have been helpful for describing what I was experiencing and feeling on a conscious and subconscious level. It was Mezirow who did groundbreaking research trying to understand why and how people change. He coined the term "transformational learning theory": basically an expensive graduate school phrase that provided a theory about how and why people change.

My disorienting dilemma had to do with what I saw and experienced in a broken East Coast city. Drug dealers populated the noisy corners where children with unlaced Adidases played. Gunshots ricocheted on humid summer evenings while young girls (out too late) jumped double Dutch, and boys soared to toss basketballs at makeshift milk-crate hoops. Teens complained about overcrowded schools and didn't bother to go; then dropped out. Unemployed adults loitered in a few unkempt parks. Streets had long since been abandoned by trash crews.

I had never been on a road like this before. My childhood had been filled with happy days in school, summer weekends playing safely; I was responsible for cutting lush, green lawn and attending tennis camp. I played golf on the manicured links. The only explosive noises in my neighborhood were from holiday firecrackers.

Immediately, the Philadelphia street scenes thrust me into that feverish and porous state described by Camus. And, of all things,

Camus claimed that that was a good position to be in if one really wanted to grow. My conflicted faith began to look different. The Bible began to read differently. My Christian clichés and platitudes had never been held against the backdrop of this obtuse inequality. Now I was being exposed to my own emptiness.

What did it mean to be a Christian in a country with such vivid, garish disparity? Where was the gentle Jesus of blessings; where was God's omnipotence and love amid such decay and hopelessness? No Bible study had ever raised these questions for me. No time spent in personal devotions had ever created my new state of vulnerability and openness. God was using this porous experience to drain me of the old and fill me with something new. But I didn't know that at first.

Interestingly, Mezirow believed there were different kinds of change. There is a change of our perspectives, and there is real transformation. A perspective change says that after being exposed to something new—new culture, new theories, new beliefs, new art—we might look at our world differently. Perspective change is important. The only problem is that it doesn't necessarily move us toward new behaviors. We might look at the world differently, but it may not change the course of our lives or the depth of our service.

ROAD MARKER

Sometimes we have to cross the road to understand how spiritually immature we really are.

According to Mezirow, there is a deeper kind of change. He calls this deeper change "real transformative learning." This change occurs less frequently. He argues that transformative learning usually begins with a disorienting dilemma: it is a life crisis. It will be an event or encounter that inverts our way of understanding reality. This disorienting dilemma ignites a period of self-examination. Following our self-examination, we will challenge our assumptions about life, circumstances, and people (for example, all inner-city kids are gangbangers; all poor people are lazy; all middle-class people are happy). Challenging our assumptions leads us to explore the possibility of new roles and new actions for our lives. Seeing ourselves in new roles helps us envision a new plan for how we might live fully transformed.

Disorienting dilemmas can jump-start a series of events that will ultimately lead to changed behavior—like a catalyst in a chemical reaction. And when those disorienting dilemmas become part of the equation for spiritual growth, the results will be dynamic and profound. There is no better place to witness this phenomenon at work than in the lives of the disciples.

JESUS' DISORIENTING DILEMMAS

It's important, right at the start, to identify the obvious truism: Jesus was no ordinary teacher. It's a shame that so many pastors and spiritual leaders reduce Jesus' life to just his words. If Jesus believed that his words alone transformed people, he would have set up a central location on one of several hills in the area and preached sermons all day. Yet the dynamism of Jesus' ministry was when he changed people—stubborn, ordinary, uneducated, sometimes unteachable people. He could have had his followers simply take notes and nod at his most salient insights. That was not Jesus' idea of effective ministry. Jesus indeed was passionate about changing the world. But changing the world, as he knew it, would take transformed people. Transforming those people would take more than hymns, meat loaf dinners, or catechism classes.

So Jesus introduced the discipline of road crossing as part of his spiritual-growth program. Take Mark's telling of the story of Jesus healing a leper. Can you imagine the utter horror and astonishment of the disciples when Jesus violated the Hebrew purity codes by touching a leper? When healthy people approached a leper, they would literally veer to the other side of the road to avoid potential contact. Separating oneself from a brush with individuals carrying that dread disease was a requirement of the law (Leviticus 13). Everybody knew that to touch a leper would be violating religious code. Jesus turned the code on its head; he got off the sidewalk and walked across the road. Talk about a disorienting dilemma.

Or imagine the confusion of the disciples when Jesus said to the badly deformed, unwashed man, "Son, your sins are forgiven" (Mark 2:5). Nowhere in the disciples' childhood training would they have learned that a traveling teacher had the authority to forgive sins. That authority was reserved for priests employed by the Temple. Talk about disorientation. Or can you imagine the embarrassment and discomfort the disciples experienced when Jesus met with reviled tax collectors and notorious sinners at Levi's house (Mark 2:15)? That was career suicide for a holy man and those associated with him. What would people think? Another disorienting dilemma. I'm only in the second chapter of Mark, and Jesus has already crossed multiple roads.

Every time Jesus confronted what was socially acceptable, or challenged what would have been a normative religious practice, or confronted the establishment, the disciples were forced to reevaluate their faith. They scratched their heads and talked worriedly among themselves. They examined and questioned their assumptions about what it meant to love God and what kinds of people were important to God. They did not fully comprehend what Jesus was doing. But each of those events, whether the disciples knew it or not at the time, left an indelible mark on their memories and etched a clearer picture of discipleship. And that is why crossing roads should be part of our spiritual practice—to jolt us awake, challenge us to ask uncomfortable questions that keep us honest, and protect us from laziness.

It is important to keep in mind that spiritual disciplines are not ends in themselves. They must lead us somewhere. They are not simply holy finger foods that provide extra calories to fatten us up spiritually, nor are they a way for us to accumulate notches on our spiritual belts. Disciplines are exercises that move us to new places, new depths, new insights, and new ways of living. They are supposed to change us.

In the case of the disciples, Jesus attempted to reframe their understanding of what it meant to *love God*. Jesus was in the business of transforming people into compassionate followers of the very God of gods. Thus, spiritual growth for the disciples involved embracing a new sense of holiness—a vision different from that which was offered by status-quo religions and politics. Jesus called his vision the Kingdom of God. He intentionally used kingdom language because it signaled a departure from the existing kingdoms that his followers understood. But he wasn't referencing the kingdom of Rome that ruled through intimidation, oppression, and military force.

ROAD MARKER

Jesus crossed the road to demonstrate the
vision of a new Kingdom.

The Kingdom Jesus espoused was very different. In Jesus' Kingdom the first were last, greatness was found in humility, enemies were forgiven, the weak were embraced and healed, and the meek would inherit the earth. That was a stark contrast for the kingdoms familiar to the people of Israel during the Roman occupation. Jesus knew that compelling his followers to embrace his vastly different vision would take more than contemplation or inhaling some aromatic incense or discussing the Torah over exotic tea. It would take a revolutionary kind of vigorous spiritual-growth program that changed both perspective and behaviors. That kind of program is needed today—if we expect real transformation to take place.

REDEFINING SPIRITUAL MATURITY

Could there be a link between crossing roads and genuine, life-transforming spiritual growth? Do encounters with people who are different from me really challenge me to grow and change in ways that familiar spiritual disciplines do not? If I decide to alter my weekly schedule, opening it up to the road-crossing actions of Jesus, will I change in ways that truly stretch my understanding of my faith and God? Yes. Engaging in the discipline of road crossing will put you and me in situations where dismissing the discomforts of growth is not an option. If road crossing becomes a vital part of our spiritual diets, it will place us in the middle of life events where there will be no escape hatches, no back doors, no falling asleep while saying our prayers, no closing our Bibles in the midst of complex or convicting passages.

If road crossing as a spiritual discipline helps prompt a process of transformation in our lives—one that moves us toward a place of spiritual maturity—perhaps we should understand what spiritual maturity actually means. The apostle Paul writes about "those of us then who are mature" (Philippians 3:15, NRSV), and those who are "alive with Christ" (Ephesians 2:5), and he says, "if anyone is in Christ, he is a new creation" (2 Corinthians 5:17). Paul goes even further when he hints that there are different levels of spiritual maturity. He writes that each of us can move from infancy to a more complete stage of faith (1 Corinthians 3:1-2). So what does maturity look like?

Over the years I have heard people refer to other Christians as people with a deep faith, spiritual giants, pillars of the church, those who are solid in their walk with God. Often these references are given to believers within a particular faith community who have garnered a kind of reputation as being further along than most of us on the faith journey road. The criteria used to "measure" the person's spiritual maturity might be related to his or her ability to preach, teach, or fluently quote Scripture. Others might add that maturity has to do with how we outwardly display the fruit of the Spirit—love, joy, kindness, self-control, etc.

Theologian Ronald Marstin has an interesting concept of the idea of spiritual maturity. Marstin sees deep faith as being more than Bible memorization or advanced degrees in theological studies. Marstin believes that true spiritual maturity includes our ability to interface with people unlike ourselves. Conclusively, Marstin argues that road crossing is not a simple activity that creates spiritual transformation, but it is the mark of a spiritually mature person. Marstin comments:

> Behind any real conversion, in other words, we should be looking for some real change in a person's social relations, some change in the kind of community with which the person feels at home. . . . [W]e should find an expansion of the range of people with whom we identify and to whom we feel responsible. The broadening vision that signals faith's maturing implies, then, a broadening of the range of people who contribute to that vision. By the same token, the limits of faith's maturity can be measured by the range of people whose experience it ignores.[2]

Spiritually mature people are road crossers—not the people who live in isolation or hide within communities of comfort. Spiritually mature people build friendships, engage in meaningful relationships, and experience community with those who are different from themselves.

We see the road-crossing pattern in the life and example of Jesus. Since Jesus was a man who fully realized his spiritual maturity, we would do well to follow his lead—certain that even the most stubborn of us will be changed.

CHAPTER THREE

CAN A ROCK REALLY CHANGE?

I see very clearly that God shows no favoritism.
In every nation he accepts those who fear him
and do what is right.

PETER, IN ACTS 10:34-35, NLT

"It is an affront to our Creator and the inerrant Holy Scriptures!" bellowed Dwayne, his ruddy facial complexion turning a deeper shade of red.

Dwayne had bitten my hook—loaded with one of the many juicy, theological worms I loved to dangle in front of him. I knew he could not swim past the bait. For Dwayne, it was as if the future of Christendom rested on preserving this truth. He looked at me square in the eye, wagged his finger, and unequivocally stated: "Women should never be ordained!" We were off and running.

Dwayne and I loved to argue. We were always creative in our sparring, enjoying every word of it.

But we made sure our arguments never became nasty and our bantering always remained within the boundaries of civility. That's because Dwayne is such a nice guy.

He worked on our staff for a number of years—dedicated, sincere, kind, compassionate, and prayerful. I could never be cantankerous for more than a moment with anyone holding those qualities.

Dwayne also served on weekends as an associate pastor at a

fairly conservative Baptist church. When he wasn't tutoring or mentoring young people, Dwayne was planning mission trips, teaching Sunday school, and preaching Sunday sermons.

Anyone like Dwayne, willing to work for pennies to stem the tide of poverty, is someone who easily earns my respect. He willingly jumped into the trenches, got dirt under his nails, rolled up his sleeves for the difficult jobs. Dwayne had my admiration and that of everyone on his team.

But even though both Dwayne and I were raised as Baptists, we often held different opinions on theological issues. He is a nice guy, but count on it: on certain issues he will not waver.

Case in point: his unswerving conviction that women should *not* be ordained. No. Never. Ever. They *could* be permitted to teach Sunday school to little children, or be missionaries in some far-off country, or speak to senior women's groups, but he never wanted them in the pulpit! Please. In case you missed his opening argument, Dwayne had the "once-for-all, delivered-to-the-saints" Holy Scriptures to support his position.

Both he and I sparred with great, intense discussions as we gulped scalding coffee at the café. Dwayne would pull out his big red leather Bible (a King James Version, of course), turn to 1 Timothy 2:12, and read aloud: "I suffer not a woman to teach, nor to usurp authority over the man." He again and again hammered home the point that the apostle Paul was consistent in reminding his followers that *men were meant* to be the spiritual head of the church. "Sure, women are allowed to serve, Bruce, but they just *cannot* have *authority* over a man. Remember, Adam was formed *first*. Not Eve."

I countered with the fact that surely he must remember that the first "preachers" of the Good News were women. On Easter Sunday morning, while the disciples were asleep (and hiding?), it was Mary Magdalene, Mary the mother of James, and Salome who were on their way to Jesus' tomb. Their biggest concern that morning was who would roll away the stone so they could get to the body and properly embalm it. But en route, in the lifting darkness, they were met by an unexpected angel, who rather affirmatively told them to go tell Peter and the other disciples that "He is risen!"

"Come on, Dwayne," I bantered. "If God was so opposed to women preachers, why would God give the most important message in the history of Christendom to a group of women?"

"But the *disciples* that Jesus chose were all men," retorted Dwayne heatedly. "If Jesus had wanted women on his team, he would have chosen them as part of his inner circle. That's biblical, Bruce. You've just got to trust the Bible," he said as passionately as a lawyer's final courtroom trial summation.

I took a long swallow of my steaming coffee before proceeding. "Dwayne," I reasoned quietly, "look at all the other biblical women who had significant leadership roles in advancing the work and witness of God in the world—Esther, Ruth, Naomi, Dorcas, just to name a few that come to mind. If God was so adamant about repressing the contribution of women in the Bible, why weren't those names eliminated from the Old Testament and just the names of men highlighted?"

Even though I knew my one-man jury wasn't with me on this one, I eloquently presented *my* closing argument. "Dwayne, times have changed. It would have been culturally unacceptable for a male teacher to include a woman as a disciple. Jesus worked within the cultural parameters of his day. Remember, Jesus lived in a patriarchal society."

"Oh, no, no, no, Bruce. Now you're using your own interpretative lens." Dwayne was nearly shouting. "If you start applying your *relativistic* pick-and-choose approach to biblical interpretation you can just about eliminate anything you want from the Bible based merely on your own subjectivity or whim!"

"Yes, but *you* do that already!" I stayed cool.

"I do not!" he shouted, making me think of Martin Luther's "Here I Stand" speech. "I take the Bible literally. It is the inerrant Word of God!!" (In Dwayne's debates, there are always lots of exclamation points.)

"Come on, Dwayne. Lighten up," I coaxed. "There are a hundred things in the Bible that *you* already dismiss because of their cultural irrelevancy. Ever have ham for your Easter dinner? Will you stone your children if they talk back to you? Should women cover their heads in church? Dwayne, you're always making subjective judgments about the Bible passages you embrace and those you don't."

After such exchanges we would call it a stalemate, both go to our corners, and regroup for our next argument. We worked well together, yet had fun respectfully disagreeing. On this one, I knew Dwayne wasn't going to change his position; losing his argument would mean surrendering everything he believed. It just wasn't going to happen.

But I wasn't going to change my position either.

Because of our similar backgrounds, I did appreciate his argument. I had also met dynamic, committed women in seminary who had sincere callings to preach and lead churches. Could I just dismiss their callings as mere delusions or misreading of a few isolated Bible verses?

You can be sure I was not about to give up on Dwayne. I had a plan.

MEETING HIS MATCH

Six blocks from our ministry headquarters is a Presbyterian church. Because the church supported our organization, I knew the staff. The associate pastor was young, single, and a woman. Janet had a great personality and loved to laugh. She also had a passion for youth ministries, for the church, and for missions. She lived out her calling with integrity and energy. She was a levelheaded, mature young woman doing a great job.

I decided to set Janet and Dwayne up on a blind date. That was all. Just a simple date. I knew Janet could handle Dwayne and maybe, since she was an astute theologian, help me win our argument. After all, it is not every day that a conservative Baptist associate pastor (who does not believe in women in ministry) goes out on a date with a progressive, ordained Presbyterian clergywoman.

Dwayne and Janet went out on my arranged date.

"How'd it go last night?" I asked Dwayne the next morning at the office. "Did you see the light yet?" I chuckled.

"No," Dwayne abruptly assured me, "I'll be the first to let you know. Umm, Bruce, she seemed like a nice person." Needless to say, I felt a little defeated. This was not the outcome I had hoped for. "Oh, by the way, Bruce," he added with a slight, sheepish grin, "we're going out again next Friday night! You don't have to arrange anything."

Friday was not their last date. They went out again. And again.

Then they announced their engagement.

Dwayne and Janet were married! I was as happy as they were.

Are you ready for God's sense of humor? The happy, delightful couple now serve together in Tajikistan—as copastors!

LOVE CHANGES EVERYTHING

It is critical to realize that Dwayne's hesitancy to change a theological position had little to do with the issue of women in the ministry. Seldom does our unwillingness to change have anything to do with the issue we find ourselves defending. I believe our reluctance to alter our positions is ultimately rooted in fear. Changing a position involves letting go of ideas and convictions that are part of a person's core identity. In Dwayne's case, his position on biblical interpretation gave him a sense of meaning and defined his identity. He was an inerrantist. His theology connected him to a certain community of faith which agreed with him and which, in turn, provided him a sense of belonging and community. In his book, there was nothing worse than a heretic. For Dwayne, change meant loss. Change could mean alienation from meaningful friendships—even the loss of his role in his church. And that's why change—a strong psychological event—is difficult for most people. Embracing a new belief can mean letting go and stepping into the abyss of uncertainty. It can mean the anchors of friends, family, and associates disappear.

ROAD MARKER

Sometimes we have to cross the road to see that people who don't hold our views can still love God.

What intrigued me about Dwayne's experience was watching him slowly shift his position on the issue of women and ordination because of the new relationship he was forming "on the other side of the road." As he developed a deeper relationship with Janet, he discovered someone who was deeply committed to God and sincerely believed that she had been called into full-time service. His theology was no longer an abstraction—she had a face, she had a heart. Within the context of a loving relationship, Dwayne was able to see beyond a few verses and consider the fact that Janet's calling could not be reduced to a trifling discussion.

Now don't shut the book if you disagree with Dwayne's new theological position. I can hear a brother or sister say, "Bruce, perhaps *you* were supposed to change *your* position! I can't get around Paul's clear verses about the role of women in the church! I never will." That critique is fair enough. But let's look at the broader issue.

My point of sharing Dwayne's story is not to launch into a lengthy discussion about Pauline theology (there are lots of great commentaries with compelling arguments) but rather to illustrate how different life can look when we are in relationship with another human being—when we get close enough to another person to *hear* his or her heartbeat and *see* life through his or her eyes. Sure, we can still disagree on certain theological or political positions, but when we allow ourselves to enter into a loving relationship with a human being who thinks and expresses him- or herself differently from us, there is a chance God can use those experiences to dramatically expand our worldview and enhance the fruitfulness of our lives and faith.

What I found interesting about Dwayne's journey was *why* and *how* he changed. First, change did not come because he doubled his dosage of the traditional spiritual disciplines, a prescription that would have reinforced his preexisting ideas. Dwayne's position changed because he crossed the road. On the other side of the road was another human being, fully made in the image of God. God can use the most unlikely relationships to bring significant change in our lives.

CAN A ROCK CHANGE?

If there was anyone in the history of Christendom who could have rested on his spiritual laurels it was the apostle Peter. By Acts chapter 10, Peter had made a complete turnaround from his earlier failure as Jesus' disciple. The beginning chapters of Acts reveal a man who preached with boldness, healed sick people, and even raised someone from the dead—impressive qualities to have on one's spiritual résumé. If I attained that level of spiritual output, I'd be inclined to put my life on cruise control. After raising someone from the dead, what could I do to top that?

In Acts 10, however, Peter underwent a remarkable transformation. It was a transformation of attitude, a conversion of *perception*. It was a dramatic revolution of his worldview. From God's perspective, Peter was not complete. Peter still needed to grow and change. Peter believed that the grace of God, the

Good News message of the gospel, was exclusive to the Jews. Although Peter didn't realize it, this thinking was a problem for God because it limited his redemptive work in the world. Peter needed to change, to grow.

Easier said than done. Since childhood Peter had observed the disciplines of his orthodox Jewish faith. He had eaten kosher food, observed Jewish traditions and the Sabbath, and had been profoundly impacted by a worldview that made distinctions between people on the basis of ethnicity.

When we meet Peter in Acts 10, he is on a rooftop at lunchtime; he is hungry. While waiting for his meal to be prepared, Peter fell into a trance. He saw something like a large sheet held by its four corners come down from heaven. The sheet was filled with animals—all kinds of animals—animals that were permitted to be eaten by Jews and animals that were forbidden to be eaten. For those of us who are not versed in the laws of Jewish orthodoxy, this vision of animals in a bedsheet does not make much sense. But the words following this strange apparition would have been absolutely earth shattering to a man priding himself on obedience and personal piety.

God said, "Get up, Peter. Kill and eat" (Acts 10:13).

"Surely not, Lord!" Peter replied. "I have never eaten anything impure or unclean" (10:14).

God spoke to Peter again—this time, I imagine, with a deep, compelling baritone voice: "Do not call anything impure that God has made clean" (10:15).

Essentially, God was saying to Peter, "The rules have been changed!"

Three times the vision came to Peter. But mind this: the real change in Peter did not come through his visions. The visions simply moved Peter toward a road that needed to be crossed. Peter's transformation actually came when he crossed the road—a road that a righteous Jew would resist crossing because it involved releasing everything that devout person would have held to be sacred and important. It meant disbanding the childhood faith that had guided him into adulthood and turning his back on the community that identified who he was and where he belonged. Peter balked at God's request. I can't say I blame him. It is never easy letting go of things we have learned in our formative years. But God wanted to radically change this fisherman—with a real spiritual DNA alteration.

Thus, the story gets even more interesting.

GENTILES LOVE GOD TOO?

Just then God had three men arrive at the front door of the house in Joppa where Peter was staying. I don't know about you, but when three uninvited people show up at my doorstep (especially at lunchtime), I get nervous. I might even be inclined to close the curtains and turn off the lights.

The men, who ask for Peter by name, want him to accompany them to the house of a Roman officer named Cornelius who lived in Caesarea, a day's trip down the Mediterranean coast. Not only was Cornelius a Roman, but of all things, he was a Gentile. But not just *any* Gentile. Cornelius had been *noticed* by God because his "prayers and gifts to the poor have come up as a memorial offering before God" (10:4). Cornelius was a devout and God-fearing man with a compassionate heart toward the poor, and he was going to play a significant role in Peter's transformation. It would be this encounter, not the vision, which would ultimately challenge Peter's limited theology.

So Peter traveled with the three strangers to Cornelius's house. Peter was embarking on a short-term cross-cultural and cross-religious mission trip. But unlike some modern mission trips, he was not going to build houses or help at an orphanage. Peter was going to have a transformational encounter with a *Gentile brother* (horrors) who had a dynamic, living, and authentic faith.

Verse 28 provides a critical and essential insight into how

profound and radical this trip would be. After arriving and being greeted reverently by Cornelius, Peter claimed, "You are well aware that it is *against our law* for a Jew to associate with a Gentile or visit him" (emphasis added). The significance of Peter's words cannot be dismissed casually. For Peter to enter Cornelius's house was tantamount to breaking the law. Not only was Peter being asked to visit a Gentile, God was asking Peter to . . . break the law. God's request of Peter might be equivalent to a devout Catholic taking Communion in a Protestant church, or a Caucasian sister inviting African Americans for dinner in Alabama during the height of the civil rights era. This was radical behavior. In an effort to change Peter, God requested Peter to break God's own law—or what was perceived to be God's law.

From Luke's careful description in Acts of what took place at Cornelius's house, we witness a dramatic transformation in Peter's life. A man who still honored the dietary laws of the Jewish faith and still acknowledged the purity laws that divided Jews and Gentiles, Peter ultimately conceded, "God has shown me that I should not call any man impure or unclean" (10:28). Peter's worldview changed. And then came Peter's "aha" moment when he boldly proclaimed, "I truly understand that God shows no partiality, but in every nation anyone who fears him and does what is right is acceptable" (10:34-35, NRSV).

ROAD MARKER

Peter crossed the road and discovered how big God's love really is.

This encounter changed the course of the fledgling Christian movement. From that point forward, Peter now realized that God's grace was not limited to people of Jewish origin. The Good News now is not simply limited to the "circumcised" (10:45), but the message of forgiveness and redemption is for all humanity. The early Christian movement dramatically shifts from a small sect within the Jewish community to a movement that embraced all humanity. That change was a radical departure from the disciples' original mission statement. Needless to say, the change initially upset "the apostles and the brothers throughout Judea" (11:1), and Peter was forced to return to Jerusalem and share his story of transformation with the Jewish believers in that city.

Peter's story is a testimony of significant change. It is also a story of the transformative power of crossing roads of difference—even when those relationships on the other side of the road challenge our most cherished traditions and beliefs. Something dynamic happened when Peter *saw* Cornelius and *heard* his story. Peter was willing to risk a journey with a few strangers that would require courage and the suspension of beliefs he held to be true. Because of Peter's change, the direction of the early Christian movement took an exciting turn. Thank God, even a *rock* can change.

SEEING THEIR FACES, HEARING THEIR VOICES

As demonstrated in Peter's life, change is often sparked by the presence of the most unlikely people—people that we would never put on our A, B, or Z list. Peter would have thought it more likely for hell to freeze over (or maybe the Sea of Galilee) before suspecting God would use a Gentile to turn his life upside down. If you had asked Peter the week before his Cornelius encounter if he believed a Gentile could teach him anything about God, about faith, or about the visionary impact of Jesus, I am sure he would have laughed at you. And yet God did all of that to broaden Peter's vision.

I have long admired the work of the philosopher Nicholas Wolterstorff. His efforts to integrate good philosophical thinking and Christian theology, and his commitment to the broader themes of social justice, have challenged me personally. As professor of philosophical theology at Yale University, he is no lightweight academic. His books *Until Justice and Peace Embrace* and *Religion in the Public Square* speak of his commitment to bridging the gap between abstract philosophical thought and the lives of ordinary people. Wolterstorff's moving story about the death of his child, *Lament for a Son,* is a classic on how a parent attempts to make sense of an untimely, premature death. Interpreting Jesus' saying, "Blessed are those who mourn," he makes, in my opinion, one of the most insightful commentaries on this verse (Matthew 5:4). Wolterstorff claims this beatitude calls Christians to be "aching visionaries"[1]—people who have caught a glimpse of what God's world should look like and mourn when they do not see that vision realized. When we see hunger, blindness, and violence, we should mourn because it falls short of what God wants for humanity.

When introduced to an author like Wolterstorff, I am always curious to understand what influences birthed his commitment to integrating faith with making the world a more just and livable place for all people. Did it come from reading certain books? If so, what books? Did it come from listening to certain preachers? If so, what preachers? Did it come from studying under certain professors? If so, what professors? What influences challenge a brilliant man to move beyond academic musings of the Ivy League and think about issues that matter to ordinary human beings?

A similar question was posed to Wolterstorff: "How did a Reformed philosopher become passionate about justice?" His answer was revelatory.

I became passionate about justice because of two episodes in my life. First, in September 1976 I attended a conference in South Africa at which not only were white Afrikaners present but also black and "colored" (mixed race) scholars from South Africa. The latter two groups spoke in moving language about the indignities daily heaped upon them and pleaded for justice. I felt that I had been called by God—in the classic Protestant sense of "call"—to speak up in my own way for these wronged people.

Second, in May 1978 I attended a conference on Palestinian rights on the west side of Chicago. About 150 Palestinians were present, most of them Christian. They too poured out their hearts about the indignities heaped upon them and pleaded for justice. Again, I felt that I had been called by God to speak up for these wronged people.[2]

Wolterstorff summarizes these two significant events in his life with biblical fervor: "In short, it was *hearing the voices* and *seeing the faces* of the wronged that evoked in me a passion for justice."[3]

When Wolterstorff talks about transformative moments in his life—changes that have altered the way he lives out his vocation—he doesn't mention sermons, prayer, worship, philosophical readings, or the scholarly study of Scripture. (I am not dismissing these disciplines as insignificant in his life; obviously those disciplines have shaped him.) Rather, his commitment to justice comes from "hearing the voices and seeing the faces" of those wronged by injustice. Human encounters—face-to-face—with the broken, the hurt, and the demonized sparked his passion for justice.

A Dutchman raised in the Reformed tradition, this brilliant philosopher could have easily lived out his academic profession indifferent to the issues of black South Africans, or remained ambivalent and uncommitted about the issues surrounding Palestinians and their relationship to Israel. He could have remained a noncontroversial Christian writer. Yet something happened when he heard the stories and saw those faces. The words of the voiceless seeped into his heart and conscience. He could no longer turn his back on people wronged by racially biased theologies or misguided government policies, because their cries forever changed his life.

In some ways, Wolterstorff's journey of change is similar to those of Peter and Dwayne. For each of these men, God used the stories of the excluded to bring them to their "aha" moments— moments challenging them to reevaluate the true meaning of their faith and alter their vocational visions.

Stories of true transformation remind me—and hopefully you—of all the exciting and dramatic potential of crossing roads. These stories also remind me that stubborn apostles, detached professors, and Bible-wielding pastors can all change. When we build friendships of love with people who think differently, have different life experiences, and express their faith convictions in new ways, the impact can be dynamic. Wolterstorff reminds us of this hope by claiming that relationships can change the way we think, the way we write, the way we live, the way we love, the way we pray, and the way we ultimately live out our faith in our vast and complex world.[4]

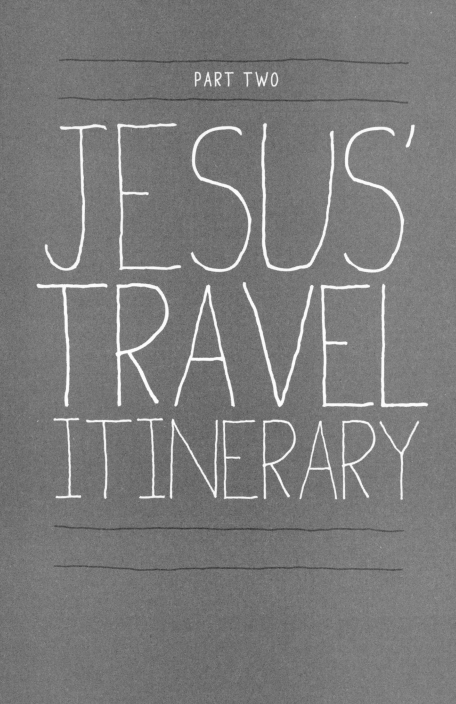

PART TWO

JESUS' TRAVEL ITINERARY

CHAPTER FOUR

CROSSING THE ROAD TO THE POOR

The challenge for the modern Christian is no matter what profession you are in, you have to stand shoulder to shoulder with the poor. . . . People in their [Mercedes] Benzes and big cars pass through here every day, but don't see behind the walls.

MONSIGNOR RICHARD ALBERT[1]

We see from where we stand.

HAITIAN PROVERB

Ryan stood on the corner of Ferry Avenue and Broadway trying to take a breath. Up to this point, he had never given the process of breathing a second thought: just inhale, exhale, inhale.

But today was different; his lungs were laboring and he was gasping. He didn't have asthma, emphysema, or another lung-related ailment. "I panicked; it was like something was lodged in my throat. I was nauseous—about to throw up," Ryan told me.

The problem was where he was standing: Ferry and Broadway, South Camden, New Jersey, on a hot August day. Few places in America have worse air quality. Local residents know better than to move far from their worn-out air conditioners in August.

Why was it so bad? Two blocks from where Ryan was standing was a raw sewage treatment plant that processes the human waste from thirty-seven affluent counties surrounding Camden.

Thousands of gallons of effluvia flow daily into Camden's broken, poor neighborhood to be treated.

If the treatment facility were located on some remote island, or in an area designated as an industrial-waste dump, the foul odor would not be a problem. But in this inner-city neighborhood, children jump rope and hopscotch; teenagers play basketball in weed-clotted, abandoned lots; and single mothers nurse babies while breathing the rancid air, presenting a significant health risk to both. But nobody notices. No one cares.

"This would *never* be allowed in any middle-class neighborhood!" barked Ryan, with all the youthful indignation he could muster. "We should invite the mayors of all the surrounding towns down for a luncheon and watch as they gag over this town. They'd never tolerate this!"

They certainly wouldn't tolerate this in *their* backyards. Any neighborhood of doctors, lawyers, and professionals would be up in arms about this basic violation of human rights—not to mention the negative impact it would have on their expensive real estate investments.[2] But when you're poor and powerless, odors and stench just happen. As the neighborhood priest said graphically, "We're the toilet bowl of New Jersey."

Ryan, working on his master's degree at a prestigious East Coast seminary, was experiencing a disorienting dilemma. He was having an experience that turned his world upside down. The contrast between the putrid smells of Ferry and Broadway and the fragrance of freshly cut lawns back at school created a spiritual short circuit for him. His two years of writing exegetical papers, parsing Greek nouns, and debating Karl Barth's eschatology seemed at the moment to be completely irrelevant to the fact that children were inhaling toxic fumes that would lead to respiratory problems and shortened life spans.

As Ryan raged about the injustices of foul air, he shouted, "Why do these conditions exist? Has anyone phoned the sewage treatment plant? Let's get someone from Congress involved." Then, "Is this God's will for the people of this community? Am I somehow complicit because I do nothing?"

Life-challenging questions can translate into actions. And that happened with Ryan. Before the end of the day, Ryan called the sewage treatment plant, the local politicians, and the Environmental Protection Agency. Before the end of the week, Ryan had made air quality for children the focus of his internship with UrbanPromise. Feverishly he unearthed incriminating data and information about the ones responsible for creating and sustaining these unconscionable circumstances. Ryan had a mission.

What sparked Ryan's awakening? What unharnessed his passionate energy toward injustice? Was it his morning prayers? Perhaps his expanded Greek vocabulary? Or his ability to debate the finer points of theologians Barth, Calvin, and Tillich? Maybe his faith-enriching studies prepared him to process what he experienced that morning on the corner of Broadway and Ferry. His seminary had provided a rich vocabulary to name sin and evil and injustice. But the moment that created a crisis was when he simply breathed the air.

ROAD MARKER

Sometimes we have to cross the road to
breathe our neighbor's toxic air.

WE "SMELL" FROM WHERE WE STAND

A pithy Haitian proverb reads, "We see from where we stand." Change the location of your feet, the proverb suggests, and you will see things differently. If we live in a gated community, for example, our view of passersby is limited by the walls that enclose us. If we shop at Banana Republic and Armani we're likely to run into people who look and dress exactly like us. If we attend a church that reflects our same demographic makeup, the world tends to look the same color.

When Ryan placed himself in the center of an impoverished, broken community and smelled the air, the scales fell from his eyes. When the scales were gone, his heart was touched. When his heart was touched, his mind began to work. And when his mind began to work, his hands and feet began to follow. This is how change takes place. This is why we need to add road crossing to our menu of spiritual disciplines. Road crossing changes those who dare to travel to the other side.

I am not naive enough to believe that every trip to a poor community is going to place us on a path of spiritual and vocational discovery. Nor do I think that simply shopping in the barrio will make us justice-oriented Christians. After twenty-five years of working in what is deemed a poor community, I can assure you there is nothing magical nor intrinsically transformative about poverty. Not every poor person is grateful, courageous, and committed. Not everyone living in poverty has some wonderful virtue to share with the affluent. Not every poor community has a stinking sewage plant.

But if we believe that part of the Christian journey involves crossing roads and encountering people who are different from ourselves, then shouldn't we build friendships with those who come from a different socioeconomic class? Jesus was intentional about crossing the road to the poor; shouldn't his followers be too?

The lay theologian and activist Ronald Marstin affirms this notion of crossing borders particularly to the poor as part of a maturing and growing faith. Marstin contends:

As long as we move habitually within the circles of privilege we are insulated from the experience of the poor.

Closed to that experience, there is no reason to anticipate that we should be touched by the expectations of the poor, instructed by their perceptions, caught up in their agenda, or drawn in any sustained fashion into the companionship of those laboring to build the just society. And yet that is what maturing in faith is all about. A moral commitment may attract us to this endeavor and even convince us that we are part of it, but, confined to our own social class, we are prisoners of our own perception of things. And, as long as we are prisoners of our own perceptions, whatever we are about will not be the building of the just society.[3]

Critical to the process of crossing roads is leaving our circles of privilege and adjusting our perceptions of the world. For example, when many people look at youth in the inner city from the outside they think that they are violent, dangerous, lazy underachievers. Our perceptions have been shaped by what we have seen on television, read in the newspapers, heard on the news. But building relationships with young people from the city can reveal a completely different scenario—determination, vision, thrift, perseverance, and an understanding of how life works. According to Marstin, changing our perception moves us to a place where we can start building a more just society. Genuine relationships with poor people help us to see life through their eyes. Their struggles and their ideas for social change can be heard without the filter of an intermediary source.

When our social relations change, there is hope, says Marstin. Traversing a different social landscape helps us become more sensitive to issues of injustice—issues that keep the poor, poor. Marstin says that "where we stand on the social hierarchy necessarily gives us our point of view, our perspective on things. From where we stand we get a certain impression of the social landscape—a sense of what is right, sensible, urgent, desirable, and dangerous."[4] When we dare to cross borders, we change our social landscape, our view of life, and our understanding of others.

As our world becomes increasingly urban, increasingly diverse, and increasingly divided between the rich and poor, there's no time to lose. Without embracing this kind of discipline it will be difficult for the church to make the needed adjustment to understand and hear the voices of those beyond their church walls. It takes both a personal commitment and a commitment from the body of Christ to accomplish it.

JESUS MODELS THE WAY

If we are looking to Jesus as a model, as one who demonstrated this pattern of road crossing, we have the right to ask the simple question: when did Jesus ever cross the road toward the poor? Here is one example:

> As [Jesus] and his disciples and a large crowd were leaving Jericho, Bartimaeus son of Timaeus, a blind beggar, was sitting by the roadside. When he heard that it was Jesus of Nazareth, he began to shout out and say, "Jesus, Son of David, have mercy on me!" . . . Jesus stood still and said, "Call him here." And they called the blind man, saying to him, "Take heart; get up, he is calling you." So throwing off his cloak, he sprang up and came to Jesus. Then Jesus said to him, "What do you want me to do for you?" The blind man said to him, "My teacher, let me see again." Jesus said to him, "Go; your faith has made you well." Immediately he regained his sight and followed him on the way. (Mark 10:46-47, 49-52, NRSV)

What I find remarkable about this passage is that Jesus, knowing that his life was coming to an end (predicted in Mark 8), stopped for a man of absolutely no social significance. One cannot get much lower on the social totem pole than a man who is blind and begs for his survival. Yet while others rebuked the man, Jesus called Bartimaeus to his side. By acknowledging and welcoming this beggar, Jesus entered the poor man's world.

ROAD MARKER

Jesus crossed the road to empower a powerless outcast.

Whereas other travelers passing Bartimaeus assumed he wanted money or scraps of food, Jesus challenges the assumption by empowering the man with the question: *What do you want me to do for you?*

That is a significant question. Jesus does not impose his agenda and preconceived notions on Bartimaeus. Instead, Jesus affirms his dignity by recognizing the only thing the beggar possesses—his voice! Can you imagine what it is like to be the recipient of people's charity month after month and year after year? Can you imagine what it would be like to have dust kicked in your face and have to pretend that you are grateful for a couple of pennies? Receiving charity from people over an extended period of time is humiliating and demeaning. Many poor people resent their dependence.

Bartimaeus does not want to beg the rest of his life. He wants to be healed. He wants to see.

When the dust settled, Jesus had crossed the road and engaged with someone who was no one to anybody. Jesus took time and gave to someone who had no worldly goods to give him in return. Jesus' willingness to engage a beggar revealed what Bartimaeus *really* wanted. Bartimaeus wanted to join the community as a full participant.

I WOULDN'T TRADE IT FOR THE WORLD

Every summer our ministry brings hundreds of high school students—primarily suburban youth—into the inner city for a week of service. One of our commitments is to allow the students to meet and get to know their peers who have grown up in the inner city. Our organization does not simply want suburban youth to *work* for the poor; we want suburban youth to *learn* from the poor.

So we set up panel discussions between the urban and suburban youth. Many of these suburban youth have never had a conversation with someone of another race or socioeconomic class. To get the conversation going we start with topics most young people find interesting—music, current events, sports, and movies. Inevitably these conversations move toward issues like race, perceptions of the city and suburbs, the drug culture, and difficulties with parents. What young people from the city and the suburbs begin to discover is that once the exterior differences are stripped away, we are much alike. We all have personal insecurities, family challenges, and communities that are riddled with drug and alcohol problems.

I vividly remember a particular panel between a large group of teens from Orlando, Florida, and our youth from Camden. At one point during the discussion, a well-tanned teen said, "I work as a supervisor at Universal Studios in Orlando. I make lots of money. People around me make lots of money. But they're empty, just empty people. But there's something inside you guys. I don't know how to describe it. You've got something that those around me do not have. If I were you, I wouldn't trade it for the world."

That insight could potentially alter the life and spiritual growth of a teen in the process of evaluating his values and future priorities. I would like to believe that the next time that teen from Florida reads or hears Jesus' words about a person gaining the whole world yet losing his or her own soul, he would remember the teens from Camden who had "something inside" them. I would like to believe that the next time this teen feels like he needs to fill the void—the emptiness—in his life with the latest electronic gadget, he might invest his resources in something that will have an eternal impact.

ROAD MARKER

Sometimes we have to cross the road to discover
what is truly valuable.

Critics might say, "This road-crossing stuff sounds like a wonderful attempt for people of means to appease their guilt by having 'contact' time with people from a different social class." We do not cross roads to appease our guilt. We do not cross roads so we can check off an exotic life experience. We cross roads to learn and grow. By placing ourselves in the midst of the poor and experiencing a little of their existence, we see with new eyes, feel with new hearts, dream with new minds, and contribute with new hands and feet. This is how change takes place.

When I meet Christians who are really making a difference in the world—people who are relieving abject poverty and improving the quality of life for others—I can almost guarantee that their passions and visions were birthed during a road-crossing experience. Their examples are ones of humility and submission. To me, this is an integral part of our faith journey and truly is what taking on the mind of Christ is all about.

CHAPTER FIVE

CROSSING THE ROAD OF RACE

"First of all," he said, "if you can learn a simple trick,
Scout, you'll get along a lot better with all kinds of
folks. You never really understand a person until you
consider things from his point of view. Until you
climb into his skin and walk around in it."

HARPER LEE, *TO KILL A MOCKINGBIRD*

"Hi, Bruce. I'm calling to invite a group of your UrbanPromise children to our company's Christmas party." I listened intently to Joel Cartwright—who ran a medium-size manufacturing business and was an occasional supporter of our programs—all the while thinking to myself, *This is unusual.*

"How many children are you talking about and when is the party?" I asked.

"Oh, just bring a busload," he replied enthusiastically. "Fifty or sixty kids would be terrific!"

I paused. . . . *Fifty or sixty children at a company Christmas party? Wow!* "What's the program?"

"We'll have an afternoon buffet at the country club, followed by a fantastic magic show. All of the employees' children will be included; it'll be great fun. Of course, the most exciting part will be when Santa arrives with a gift for each of the kids. Oh, and speaking of Santa, I'll need a list of your children's names so we can get the gifts personally wrapped and tagged." I was hooked.

As Joel filled in the details, it began to sound like a great afternoon. "The kids'll love it, Joel." Actually, I had been promising our children a special treat for Christmas. Accepting Cartwright's offer would save our ministry some real money. Free food! Free entertainment and a personal gift for each kid! For urban youth ministries on low budgets, offers like that do not get any better. Merry Christmas, everyone!

"Oh, but one more thing . . . and this is confidential, Bruce," added my benevolent friend. "My business partner, Jim, adamantly opposes the idea of mixing two very different sorts of kids. I don't think there will be any outward hostility, but I just wanted to give you a heads-up. A lot of our folks have pretty negative perceptions of the inner city . . . fights, stealing, dirty kids with poor manners . . . that sort of thing."

So there *was* a catch. Cartwright was about to throw me in the middle of a power struggle between himself and his partner. Why? Why would he want to push the envelope at his company? Why would he want to jeopardize working relationships? Not many business owners would take that kind of risk.

I was faced with a decision. On the one side the party would be a potentially great time for our children; on the other side there could be a potentially explosive scene at the country club. At Christmastime. The press would love it.

But ultimately, I guessed, it was Cartwright's problem. He was the one committed to the event, the person who wanted to bring our two worlds together in the spirit of Christmas. So I accepted.

Two weeks later I pulled our big rumbling school bus through the country club gates while saying a little prayer: *Lord, give the kids a great afternoon.* The trip there had been entertaining. Sixty fourth-through-sixth graders had sung every Christmas carol imaginable. They even made up twenty new verses to "Go, Tell It on the Mountain," dragging it out for about twenty miles. My favorite stanza, spontaneously created by fifth-grader Carl Johnson, made it fun and personal:

There were some kids from Camden, freezing in a bus.
They prayed for the broken heater, but didn't make a fuss . . .
Oooooo . . . Go tell it on the mountain, over the hills
  and everywhere,
Go tell it on the mountain that Jesus Christ is born.

"May I have everyone's attention? Attention, everyone," I bellowed after I had parked the bus. "Just remember, we are guests. So be sure to say please and thank you. Now, let's have a terrific time." With those brief instructions, two other staff members, the kids, and I quietly crept into the country club in hushed awe.

As Joel promised, the food was spectacular. At the end of each buffet line was a chef in a white linen jacket—complete with ornate monogram—carving generous portions of roasted turkey and prime rib. The children weren't intimidated. They loaded their plates with piles of mashed potatoes, French fries, and Jell-O salad as if they ate like this every day. I think some of them even ate their carrots.

Eleven-year-old Tyric told me that he had made three trips to the "doctor"; he called everyone who wore a white linen coat and latex rubber gloves a doctor!

Oh, and then there were the desserts! (It was Christmas! Let your imagination fill up the plate.)

"Boys and girls, and you adults too, it's time for the magician." The excitement was palpable. Children from the inner city and those of the company employees sat cross-legged and intermingled in a half circle on the floor. It quickly became apparent which group had the most enthusiasm.

ROAD MARKER

Sometimes we have to cross the road to experience
how little it takes to give children sheer joy.

With each magic trick our Camden children inched closer to the gentleman in the black suit and top hat. Soon the magician was so sandwiched against the wall that he needed to move the eager, captivated crowd back a few feet. Each time a rabbit, dove, or multicolored handkerchief appeared, there was an eruption of laughter and wild applause. I doubt that the magician had ever performed for such an attentive and appreciative audience.

Finally, Santa Claus ho-ho-hoed his way into the midst of the joyous affair as the crowd erupted into cheers. Not only were there gifts for every child, but each gift had a name tag—no child was left out. In fact, each child was personally called to the front by Santa's assistant.

This was gift giving like none I had ever experienced. When the name of a Camden child was called to receive his or her gift, all fifty-nine of the other city children shared in the excitement by chanting in perfect cadence the name of the recipient: "Johneee, Johneee." Next it was LaToya . . . "LaaaToya." Talk about enthusiastic affirmation! I could see that even the adults in the room were amazed at the childlike wonder and exuberance the city kids expressed. But when the employees' children were called to receive their gifts, you could have heard a napkin drop. It was dead silent.

Why are the Camden kids showing such solidarity of spirit? I thought to myself. Perhaps kids bond when they grow up with limited possessions in a city renowned for its negative reputation.

The afternoon eventually came to an end. As our children finally and reluctantly got on the bus with their new toys and Styrofoam boxes filled with extra slices of prime rib and cups of ambrosia salad, they voiced their appreciation. "That was a blast!" "I can't wait to tell my mother!" "My little brother is going to love this food!" "Thanks, Mr. Main, for inviting us." Exhausted but full, the children would have stories to share at home about their day at the country club.

The next day I was sitting in my office when our receptionist, Maria, buzzed. "There's a call on line one for you."

"Bruce, it's Joel Cartwright. I just wanted to tell you what a wonderful time we all had with your children. Thanks for bringing them! Everybody enjoyed their enthusiasm and appreciated their excitement. Your kids really added something special to the party this year."

"So everything's okay?"

"Better than okay," he continued. "You wouldn't believe what happened afterward. My partner came up to me and apologized. He said he was wrong and told me that when I told him that I had invited children from Camden, he thought I was nuts. Before the party, he told our employees to hide their purses. After it was over, he thanked me for opening his eyes; he wants to get more involved in your work. In my twenty years of working with Jim, I have never heard him make that kind of confession."

A FIRST STEP

Joel Cartwright crossed a road that afternoon by extending a hand of hospitality to our children—children of a different race, different culture, and different economic class. He crossed all kinds of barriers and took a risk. If he had just wanted to do something nice for our children, he could have made arrangements to rent Chuck E. Cheese for the afternoon or thrown a wonderful pizza party. But Cartwright had a different vision. He wanted to bring two very different groups of people together face-to-face.

Someone could make a valid argument that it was a generous gift, but what did it really do for poor kids from the city? It only changed their surroundings for a moment; it didn't really change their lives. The kids still had to go back to the same dangerous, broken neighborhoods they woke up to every day. If Cartwright really wanted to make a difference, he would have invested some of his resources in the community where these children live, promoting some kind of long-term change. If he really cared about the city, he would move his business into one of the neighborhoods and employ the parents of these children—providing jobs and hope! What does feeding some African American children prime rib and ice cream and giving them toys do to promote racial equality?

These are legitimate questions. I have heard them all and spent long hours in dialogue trying to find appropriate responses. I don't dismiss the truth in these comments. But I have also been around long enough to know that it is easy to criticize someone who *does* something. Do nothing and no one complains. Do *something*—anything—and people will be quick to criticize. Even in the story of the Good Samaritan, questions could be raised about what good his compassionate act really accomplished. Jesus doesn't say whether or not the Samaritan addressed the root causes of the crime committed on the road from Jerusalem to Jericho. Did he go back and lobby Jerusalem politicians for better roads, the installation of streetlamps, and increased funding for police patrols?

ROAD MARKER

Sometimes we have to cross the road and
not worry about the consequences.

Sometimes we just need to do what we can do at the moment and not become paralyzed by the larger issues. Joel Cartwright did what he thought was right, and the perceptions of hundreds of employees were changed. Opportunities for dialogue about issues of race and cultural differences opened up around the office. Company leaders considered ongoing conversations about making their company more socially responsible and engaged in the broader community. It was a small step. But that is how large movements of change begin. Someone is willing to create a situation that gets people thinking in new and creative ways. And when people think in new and creative ways, anything is possible.

JESUS THROWS OUT THE RACE CARD

Jesus crossed borders and challenged barriers. I can think of no better example than his encounter with the Samaritan woman in John's Gospel. In this one encounter Jesus crossed at least three roads that were considered taboo for an orthodox Jewish holy man. But part of Jesus' mission was to challenge social barriers that created hatred and mistrust among people.

> Now [Jesus] had to go through Samaria. So he came to a town in Samaria called Sychar, near the plot of ground Jacob had given to his son Joseph. Jacob's well was there, and Jesus, tired as he was from the journey, sat down by the well. It was about the sixth hour. When a Samaritan woman came to draw water, Jesus said to her, "Will you give me a drink?" (His disciples had gone into the town to buy food.) The Samaritan woman said to him, "You are a Jew and I am a Samaritan woman. How can you ask me for a drink?" (For Jews do not associate with Samaritans.) (John 4:4-9)

To appreciate the radical nature of this encounter, it is critical to understand the history of conflict between the Jews and the Samaritans. The Samaritans had both hindered the rebuilding of Jerusalem after the Babylonian exile and aided Syria in fighting the Jews. The Jews had burned down the Samaritan temple on Gerizim in 128 BC. Years of mutual hostility existed between the two groups. Beyond the historical tensions, Samaritans were also viewed as racially inferior to their more orthodox Jewish counterparts. Samaritans were a mixed race, the result of generations of mixed marriages. In a culture that equated purity of race with a form of godliness, it is no wonder that the religious leadership in the Jewish community was intent on keeping those groups separate.

On this particular day, rather than heeding social expectations of devout Jews, who avoided Samaritans at all costs, Jesus took the route from Judea to Galilee less traveled by his religious counterparts. That route went *through* Samaria (John 4:3-4) instead of the longer and more difficult detour through Perea. What cannot be overlooked is the fact that Jesus did not simply avoid Samaritan territory; he went there and then struck up a conversation with one of the locals. Even more shocking was the fact that the local was a woman—even she was caught off guard when Jesus spoke to her.

New Testament scholar Judith Gundry-Volf points out that "Jesus' request for a drink of water, therefore, is deceptively simple. To make it, he had to cross great gulfs—geographical, ethnic, religious, and gender in nature."[1] Another scholar, Brenda Salter McNeil, adds that a Jew who walked in the shadow of a Samaritan was considered unclean.[2] It seems obvious that Jesus was not concerned with the social ramifications of his actions.

In two dramatic ways Jesus challenged the racial bias of his culture. First, he crossed a despised country's border; then he proceeded to ask not just a Samaritan for help, but a Samaritan *woman*. Jesus crossed the gender barrier. No Jew (especially a rabbi) would have dared to address a woman. And notice that Jesus did not command her to give him a drink of water or treat her with disdain, as if she were inferior to him. Jesus placed himself at her mercy by asking for her help. John's inclusion of this story in his Gospel confirms that Jesus' approach was radically different from the perspective of the general culture.

ROAD MARKER

Jesus crossed the road because someone
was thirsty for living water.

But there is another subplot to the story. As Gundry-Volf points out, "She comes to draw water at the sixth hour, or in the middle of the day, counting from 6 A.M. She does not come in the morning or evening, when others would be drawing water, but at the hottest time of the day. She seems to be trying to avoid social contact."[3] What was it about this woman that would compel her to go to the well at such a strange time? Her choice of living with a man outside of marriage certainly was a determining factor.

When the woman asked Jesus, "How can you ask me for a drink?" it was the perfect segue for Jesus to talk about *living water*. In probably a matter of minutes, the woman accepted Jesus' offer of living water. "Sir, give me this water so that I won't get thirsty and have to keep coming here to draw water" (4:15).

The unnamed woman was able to abandon her skepticism (4:11-12) and experience inclusion through Jesus' dismantling of ethnic, religious, and gender barriers. She desired the promise that Jesus offered.

I especially like the ending of this story. Other Samaritans in the village came to believe in God "because of the word of the woman who testified" (4:39, NKJV). "The one whom they had marginalized was now become the one through whom they believe.[4] In addition, the Samaritans pressed Jesus "to stay with them" (4:40). Jesus, a Jewish traveler crossing through Samaria to Galilee, ended up in the welcoming arms of his antagonists. Skepticism had given way to Christian hospitality, on behalf of the Samaritans, in the deepest sense. Jesus ended up staying a few days. He accepted their offer, "and because of his words many more became believers" (4:41).

What happened in Samaria is road crossing in its truest form. Jesus' actions were as radical in his day as it would be for an affluent Korean Christian today to intentionally drive into a barrio, stop where a drug dealer is hanging out, and ask for a cup of coffee. We need to be as radical as the Jesus we claim to follow.

Jesus did not insulate himself from the diversity of the world. He did not limit his travels to communities and neighborhoods that were deemed acceptable by the establishment. Jesus tackled the issues of race and ethnicity by including the places where people who didn't fit the cultural norm lived. Because of Jesus' commitment to that kind of lifestyle, he provided a challenging model of engagement for his followers.

WE'RE IN THIS TOGETHER

Jesus' behavior is a model applauded by people who want to understand the makeup of individuals who make a difference in our world. In a book called *Common Fire: Leading Lives of Commitment in a Complex World*, Laurent A. Parks Daloz and his colleagues have studied numerous adults in their forties who live intentionally committed to the common good—a good broader than simply looking after their own needs. Whether these individuals work on environmental issues, have developed socially conscious companies, work in homeless shelters, provide medical-relief services in third-world countries, or are advocates on behalf of oppressed people, the study attempts to understand what events led to the development of these committed lives. The researchers were surprised by a commonality they discovered:

> The single most important pattern we have found in the lives of people committed to the common good is what we have come to call *a constructive, enlarging engagement with the other*. . . . We had not anticipated this finding, but early in the study as people told us their stories, we began to hear about important encounters with others significantly different from themselves.[5]

Intrigued with this emerging pattern, the group looked more closely at how this "engagement with the other" actually influenced patterns of commitment. Realizing that the concept of tribe is a critical aspect in human evolution and is at the core of our social identity, the research team noticed that those who lived extraordinary lives of commitment were somehow able to move beyond tribal bonds.

They are able to engage with people of other tribes as full human beings, enlarging rather than relinquishing their networks of belonging. Having practiced compassion across tribal boundaries, sometimes nourished by the circumstances of marginality, they have come to a deeply held conviction that *everyone counts.*[6]

The Christian community can learn from these insights. To have the ability to expand "networks of belonging" and "practice compassion across tribal boundaries" is certainly important for someone who wants to develop a mature faith.

It is important to realize, however, that mere engagement with people of other tribes does not guarantee that lives will be transformed. Every day we have contact with all kinds of people who represent other tribes. These interactions may take place at the gas station, in the shopping mall, or on the bus traveling to work. Yet most of those interactions fail to produce increased empathy and commitment to the greater good. Moreover, these experiences can often be negative and even lead people to build bigger and thicker tribal walls. For the encounters to take on the status of what some social scientists would call constructive engagement, the quality of those encounters must be examined.

Parks Daloz's colleagues delved into that deeper meaning.

As we sifted through dozens of accounts, it became apparent that what distinguished a simple encounter from a constructive *engagement* was that some threshold had been crossed, and people had come to feel a *connection* with the other.[7]

Other researchers, such as Mary Watkins, refer to this feeling of connection as a "sympathetic identification."[8] In order for growth to occur in the road crosser, there must be a deeper connection made with the individuals involved in the encounter. Perhaps this is why Jesus asks questions when he engages people outside of his tribe. Asking questions and then listening is the gateway to understanding the lives of others.

ROAD MARKER

Sometimes we have to cross the road to care
about someone who is not from our tribe.

This ability to move between tribes—feeling at home in multiple worlds—is held by the person who does not live bound by the shackles of limited perspectives or immobilized by the fear of difference. This person can make an impact in the world that continues to polarize around issues of race, religion, and class. Parks argues that the kind of citizens we need to function within the complex social and ecological realities of the twenty-first century are people who can easily cross borders. Cornel West picks up on this theme in his book *Race Matters*. West champions the need for "race-transcending prophets,"[9] especially within his people group, the African American community. These are persons "who never lose contact with their own particularity, yet refuse to be confined to it."[10]

Jesus modeled for his followers in the first century the kind of behavior twenty-first-century social theorists affirm as critical for the development of more committed people and a healthier, more cooperative planet. Perhaps this is because Jesus saw people through the eyes of God—a vision of humanity not rooted in human distinctions of either race or class, but a vision of humanity made in the image of God. Jesus' mission becomes our mission as we seek to live as faithful Christians in this period of history.

MORE THAN PRAYER

It was a regular Sunday morning at Magnolia Presbyterian Church. The flowers had been arranged beautifully on the Communion table. The organist had performed a wonderful rendition of Bach's "Ach bleib' bei uns, Herr Jesu Christ." The pastor had made his opening remarks, and it was now time for the prayer of confession. I looked at the printed type and audibly followed the voice from the pulpit:

> Loving God, we admit to attitudes that exclude rather
> than embrace. We prefer to associate with others who
> think and act as we do. We turn away from those who
> are different from us. We identify some as enemies
> to be avoided or even destroyed. Forgive us, God, for
> seeking to limit your family. Awaken us to the limits of
> our understanding and the narrowness of our dealings.
> Show us the better ways you intend and make us bold
> to respond, we pray in Jesus' name. Amen.

As I looked around the sanctuary I was struck by the fact that nobody laughed or blushed in embarrassment. The pews were filled with people who all looked the same, talked the same, ate the same foods, read the same newspapers, and shared the same values. The sanctuary was a homogenous microcosm of sameness. Sure, there were men in blue suits and others in grey suits, some with striped ties, others with solid-color ties, but overall it was a very limited and incomplete picture of the family of God. Sadly, I had been visiting that church once a year for over fifteen years and *nothing had changed*. Like an old photo, the people were static. In another fifteen years, would the congregation still look the same? Would there be any difference in who sat in the pews?

The stark reality is that nothing changes unless congregations and followers of Jesus intentionally embrace the spiritual discipline of crossing roads. Prayers of confession do not lead to change. They are simply words that make us feel good because it is "Christian" to make those kinds of statements and think those thoughts. Only when we venture out of our sacred cocoons and build relationships of difference will our prayers of confession come to life. "The limits of our understanding and the narrowness of our dealings" will be expanded.

As I sat in the pew I could not help but think of two news events that had occurred the week before. Two explosive stories shocked the nation, underscoring the fragility of race relations in this country. Radio disc jockey Don Imus was fired for making racially and sexually charged comments about the Rutgers women's basketball team. Television and radio stations were all voicing their opinions about what should happen to the MSNBC radio personality, but the damage had been done. It was two steps backward for race relations, one step forward for media ratings. Almost simultaneously the men's lacrosse team at Duke University was being acquitted from charges that they raped an African American woman who had been hired as a stripper at one of their frat parties.

Both stories involved young people, many still in their teens. Both stories involved ignorance, displaying insufficient understanding and sensitivity of other communities. As one of the players on the women's basketball team commented, "Why would a man call us those kinds of names without ever taking the time to know who we were?" In one simple statement, that college freshman underscored the significance of Jesus' message. The reality: Don Imus would not have made those statements had he met the talented, hardworking, intelligent women of the Rutgers team.

The time to start dealing with racial differences is not at the moment of crisis. The way to start dealing with issues of race is by slowly cultivating friendships that move across lines of race and ethnicity. Friendships create trust. Trust creates an environment of honesty in which difficult issues can be discussed without labeling people as racists and bigots.

In the end, the Samaritans were delighted that Jesus crossed the road. After a couple of meals together, the Samaritans did not want their new friend to leave their village. Animosity and distrust had all but disappeared, and the seeds of friendship had been planted.

I am so glad Jesus did not simply pray about race relations. I am glad Jesus lived with his feet on the ground and allowed his feet to take him places where others would not go.

CHAPTER SIX

CROSSING THE ROAD OF
SPIRITUAL EXCLUSIVITY

*The curses of the ungodly are more pleasing to God's
ears than the hallelujahs of the pious.*

ATTRIBUTED TO MARTIN LUTHER

It was the first really hot day in Philadelphia. One of those early
May days that wipes out any hope that spring might extend
past Memorial Day—a sweltering reminder that the late days of
August were just a scant three months away.

The Reverend Tim Safford had slipped onto a nearly empty
bus on the corner of Second and Market, heading downtown for
a meeting. Unfortunately, like always, the bus's air-conditioning
had not been turned on and Rev. Safford quickly began fanning
himself to move a little air. Without any additional bodies on the
bus the heat was still tolerable.

But Bus 226 was running late. Consequently the crowds at
each stop were double their usual size. At each stop the bus
became more crowded . . . and the temperature began to rise.

At about Twelfth and Market a woman got on the bus, shouting into her cell phone. With one glance everyone knew more
about her than they probably wanted to know: she was an exotic
dancer in an unflattering body-hugging dress and stilettos.
Though fascinated, Tim tried not to stare. *After all, I'm a man of
the cloth,* he reminded himself. But his curiosity won out.

61

"I'm nine weeks pregnant," the stripper shouted into the phone—information the other work-bound passengers didn't need or want to know. Her voice grew louder as she screamed something about needing to take a paternity test. "It's your baby!" she cried, oblivious to the others on the bus. "You'd better take some responsibility for this one!"

That was just the warm-up act—the four-letter expletives spewed off her tongue like raging, dirty water over a dam as she walked down the aisle searching for an empty seat. With each step, the woman painted a more grotesquely personal—and colorful—picture of her tragic life.

"I'm glad I wasn't wearing my collar," mused Tim, half joking with the congregation as he relayed the experience. It was Sunday morning, and the crowd of Episcopalians needed a little levity to help swallow the pill their pastor was about to deliver.

"I watched everybody on the bus pull their newspapers closer to their foreheads, hoist their BlackBerries up to their noses, and turn up the volume on their iPods. I thought to myself, *I could do the same, and people wouldn't think I was a bad person.*

According to Rev. Safford, by the time the bus crept to Market and Seventeenth Streets it was packed and stiflingly hot. What happened next actually diffused some of the tension that had been building. "When the dancer finally took a seat, a sign above nearly shouted, 'PREGNANT? *Need help?* Call 1-800-GetHelp.'" The congregation let out a collective, though guarded, laugh to relieve a little of their anxiety. Were they supposed to be amused or shocked by this woman?

The lectionary reading that morning had been from Ezekiel. "I saw a great many bones on the floor of the valley, bones that were very dry. [The LORD] asked me, 'Son of man, can these bones live?'" (Ezekiel 37:2-3). I was curious to see how our pastor was going to connect the biblical passage to the exotic dancer, but it quickly became evident: dry bones meant lifeless people. The woman cursing on Bus 226 was living in a valley where there was not much life—just chaos, alienation, and pain. She needed to experience what the people of God have to offer.

When the dancer walked past the open seat beside Tim, he was more than a little thankful that she didn't sit down. He did not look her in the eye, offer her a word of comfort, or even mouth a silent prayer. When his stop was announced, Tim quickly disappeared out the side door.

ROAD MARKER

Sometimes we have to cross the road and quietly listen
to someone else's loudly expressed problems.

"God is not through with me yet," he shared with the somber congregation. "But what would we do if she walked in here right now? Would we escort her out? Show her the door? Or would we invite her to stay and experience the Source of Life—the one who heals, transforms, and renews?

"Church is not a fortress that protects us from the world. The church is a community of people who open their arms to all people in the loving name of Christ—wherever they are on their journey of faith."

It was refreshing to hear such transparency from the pulpit. I usually hear sermons that are filled with information to help me think more correctly about my faith or understand a biblical passage more accurately. But honestly, those sermons are easy to dismiss. I have learned that correct thinking, or even correct biblical interpretation, does not necessarily lead to compassionate action.

On this particular Sunday morning I think we were all challenged to ask ourselves a very real question: what would we do when we met our "exotic dancer" (fill in the blank) living in the valley of the dry bones? Would we take the time to embrace him or her like a brother or sister, inviting that person to the fountain of living water? Or would we be repulsed because his or her behavior violated what we have come to worship and call appropriate Christian conduct?

I wish I could say that I would respond in a way that captures the heart of God. But I cannot say that with confidence. Thank goodness God's not through with me yet. That is truly good news.

BEYOND RULES—TOWARD GRACE

A foulmouthed, promiscuous, ostensibly poor exotic dancer is a tough person for upright church folk to cross the road (or cross the aisle) and embrace. Let's face it: she embodied about every "sin" most Christians work hard to resist. Perhaps that's why we would have such difficulties with her. She is what we all try so hard not to become. Most believers make it a priority to keep their sexual appetites in check. We work hard to keep foul language to a minimum, especially at church finance meetings. We speed by striptease clubs, believing that those places are not the best environments for nurturing spiritual growth. And we try to conceive our children within marriage. These are some of the biblically based moral nonnegotiables.

So does associating with an exotic dancer, in any way, constitute leaning toward the dark side of our natures?

I think faith, for many Christians, is understood more in terms of *not* doing certain behaviors, rather than *doing* certain things. Call it guilt, church upbringing, or our understanding of God, but we tend to think God is going to *get* us for our misstep. The trouble is that following that line of thinking, faith becomes an exercise in *avoidance*, as opposed to an exercise of *engagement*. Our faith is reduced to a game of operating within a certain set of social expectations prescribed by our religious leaders and peers: you keep the rules, you keep your membership in "the club." Church becomes like any other social group—providing identity within a community of peers with certain expectations and rules. Whenever we cross the road to someone who does not live by our group's standards—like a foulmouthed exotic dancer—our place in the group is questioned. "These people are dangerous," someone might say. "They could corrupt you."

But before we pretend she doesn't exist and hide behind our newspapers or keep our eyes glued to the games on our iPhones, perhaps we need to look more closely at Jesus. Jesus was never stopped in his tracks by what those who maintained the moral and religious codes in his community thought. Whether Jesus was deemed in or out with the religious establishment was of little consequence to him. Jesus' primary motivation was to demonstrate the love and acceptance of God to all people. His identity was defined by his relationship with God, not by the reactions of his peers. His freedom allowed him to challenge the teaching and beliefs that many held to be sacred. It allowed him to cross the road.

JESUS BREAKS THE RULES

At the core of Jewish religion was what many scholars call the politics of holiness. The Jewish religious establishment had come up with a system that graded people on their purity. Where a person stood on the purity ladder made the difference in whether he or she was welcomed or excluded from the community of faith. On the top rung were Jewish men in good health with sufficient bank accounts. They were automatically considered righteous. Among the impure were the poor, the sick, Gentiles, women, and those Jews considered sinners for not keeping the law.

Jesus' frequent references to prostitutes and tax collectors should be understood in his cultural context. Prostitutes and tax collectors were among the biggest sinners in the first-century Jewish purity system. It was not a coincidence that Jesus welcomed those very outcasts and told them stories explaining clearly that God's love was extended to them too. He emphasized that maintaining the rules of the purity system was not necessarily free admission into the Kingdom of God, even if the law-abiding Jews heralded their first-in-line status from the synagogue steps. Jesus understood the true nature of God and how faith in him works: the core of real faith is not built around meeting certain rules and restrictions (most often biased toward the favored group), but is based in love and reconciliation with God and people—all people.

Jesus knew God's graciousness and understood the appropriate response of those living in right relationship with him—they were people who crossed roads even if it ruined their reputations. Why did Jesus cross roads? Because of God's love. And when he crossed the barriers between healthy and sick people, Jesus offered hope to those with little chance to cross back into the world of the redeemed. It was only by crossing into the world of the sick and sinning that Jesus was able to bring them back to the side of abundant life.

ROAD MARKER

Jesus crossed the road to save those who were lost.

Perhaps Jesus' most wonderful example of crossing the establishment's religious barriers took place on the morning he found a group of upright religious leaders ready to stone a woman for her moral failings. The apostle John writes:

> The teachers of the law and the Pharisees brought in a
> woman caught in adultery. They made her stand before
> the group and said to Jesus, "Teacher, this woman
> was caught in the act of adultery. In the Law Moses

commanded us to stone such women. Now what do you say?" They were using this question as a trap, in order to have a basis for accusing him. (John 8:3-6)

Jesus was confronted with a choice. Would he cross the road and embrace the woman—defend her, stand up for her, protect her? Or would he distance himself from her by hiding behind some religious law? After all, defending her would create conflict, enemies, and ostracism, and eventually cost him his life. (And we know how that part of the story ended.)

But Jesus stooped down and wrote in the dust with his finger. They kept demanding an answer, so he stood up again and said, "All right, but let the one who has never sinned throw the first stone!" (John 8:6-7, NLT)

We do not know what Jesus wrote for those upright, religious types to read that morning—there are numerous speculations. But we do know that he challenged a religious system that endorsed the killing of women caught in adultery. (Men were not held to the same level of accountability. Yet a woman "caught in the act" of adultery had to have a partner in crime.) In one barrier-crashing, road-crossing act, Jesus stood up for a woman with moral shortcomings. Jesus challenged a sacred law of Moses—calling into question centuries of biblical interpretation. And Jesus directly called into question the religious leaders of his day—challenging their understanding of God's heart and his intent.

When the accusers heard this, they slipped away one by one, beginning with the oldest, until only Jesus was left in the middle of the crowd with the woman. Then Jesus stood up again and said to the woman, "Where are your accusers? Didn't even one of them condemn you?" "No, Lord," she said. And Jesus said, "Neither do I. Go and sin no more." (John 8:9-11, NLT)

It's easy to speculate that many people in the crowd would have interpreted Jesus' act as being "soft on sin." Can you imagine the conversations at the synagogue that week? "What message is this sending to our young girls in the community—that it's *okay* to go around having sex whenever you want?" "This is how it always begins, a slippery slope into the pit of hell. What's next? Eating pork on the Sabbath?" "I always knew that Jesus character was a liberal."

The biblical account doesn't give any details of the stir Jesus created. But when he challenged laws and rules that people deemed sacred, Jesus demonstrated that laws and regulations are not at the heart of faith. At the heart of our faith is a compassionate God who loves human beings and believes the most despicable scoundrel can be transformed into someone beautiful.

The poignant part of John's redemptive story is that Jesus affirmed the woman, protected her, and welcomed her back into the community. First, the words of affirmation: "Neither do I condemn you." Can you picture the look on the woman's face? Then his challenge to her: "Go and sin no more."

The difference between how Jesus dealt with the woman and how the religious leaders wanted to deal with her was that Jesus first *included* her. She was not told, "Clean up your act, and then I'll protect you." Nor was she rebuked or verbally scolded. She was simply told that as far as he was concerned she was *not* condemned. Jesus' first move was to let her know that he didn't abide by the religious establishment that had excluded her. Then from a place of unconditional inclusion, the woman heard Jesus' gentle reminder to go and sin no more. What a loving difference.

Living by a fear-based faith that is more concerned with

maintaining the approval of those who hold power than in demonstrating God's love is unhealthy. As we cross the road to those the church turns its back on, we will learn and grow in our own faith. We will begin to understand the God who finds the "curses of the ungodly . . . more pleasing . . . than the hallelujahs of the pious."[1]

GRACE AT THE 7-ELEVEN

A few years ago our faith community had to reevaluate what we hold to be sacred. The story began across the street from my office in the 7-Eleven.

"Is that Violette Ngn?" I wondered aloud as I pushed my cart through the narrow aisles. "No, it couldn't be." I glanced over the top of the snack displays. At the checkout counter stood a fragile-looking young woman struggling with several bottles of baby formula and a huge pack of Huggies. Her jet-black hair was longer than I remembered, and she looked like she had gained some weight—was she pushing a stroller?

I grabbed a cold soda and walked toward her. "Violette?" She turned and forced a smile. The innocent preadolescent smile that I remembered was gone. Her dark eyes that once had danced with hope and dreams shifted toward the floor.

"Violette, it's so good to see you!"

"It's good to see you too, Mr. Main," she said flatly, trying to block the items on the checkout counter.

It had been a year and a half since I had last seen Violette; it had been at the ministry's spring teen leadership retreat. What immediately came to my mind was how much fun Violette had had playing charades; she always pushed to the front of the group, acting crazy and making everyone laugh. At sixteen, she had had drive, focus, and a growing interest and commitment to her Christian faith. Violette was bright and had talked about going to medical school. "Don't worry about me," she'd say.

As a young woman growing up in a poor home with immigrant,

Buddhist parents, she had tremendous odds to overcome. Yet her enthusiastic attendance in our after-school programs, small Bible study groups, and leadership development programs indicated that she was poised to impress us all.

Then Violette became pregnant and dropped out of school.

It is a tragic statistic that Camden, New Jersey, has one of the highest unwed teen pregnancy rates in the country at 80 percent. No one raises an eyebrow anymore when teens talk about getting pregnant. Children are raising children here.

Yet Violette had been different; we all *knew* that she would survive the daily sexual gauntlet of temptation. She had the will and focus to persevere, to beat the system.

"What are you doing these days?"

"Nut'n much."

"What do you mean? Aren't you going to school?"

"Nah. No time."

"Where are you living?" I continued as we moved toward the parking lot.

"Living?" She paused, uncertain whether she wanted to divulge more. "I . . . umm . . . I'm living in the basement of my boyfriend's house." I easily conjured up an image of tiny, depressing basement accommodations. "My parents kicked me out."

"Are you working?"

"No, I just stay in . . . watch TV . . . and care for the ba—"

"The baby?" I cut in, looking in the stroller and making all the cheery clucking sounds you do for a newborn.

"She's . . . she's doing well . . . I guess." Violette, bit by bit, began to share the gritty details of her bleak situation: her boyfriend was never around; his mother was seldom friendly to her; the colicky baby cried nonstop. Violette was trapped in a dark, cramped basement, caring for an unhappy child while learning parenting skills from *The Jerry Springer Show*.

I gently asked why she hadn't returned to visit the ministry.

Long story short, she was embarrassed. She had a deep sense of shame that she had fallen short of the community mores articulated by our dedicated staff and volunteers. In her mind, she had failed. As we talked, it became clear that Violette's energizing optimism was gone. The expression—actually the lack of expression—on her face indicated that all her hope had vanished.

"Violette, I just had a great idea! Would you be interested in becoming our volunteer receptionist? You know, answering the phones and taking messages."

"You *really* mean that?" There was a momentary glint in her eyes. "You'd like *me* to answer the phones?"

"Absolutely! Be at the office tomorrow morning by 9 A.M. Bring the baby if you can't find a sitter."

Sure enough, Violette showed up early the next morning to answer phones—without the baby. "Her father's mother said she'd watch her when I went to work," she happily explained. Violette arrived every morning for the next two months . . . on time and ready to work. She was being transformed before our eyes. Reconnecting with her community of faith provided her with a place to find healing, grow in confidence, and regain a sense of purpose.

SACRED COWS

The staff's reaction to Violette's return to our community was expected, but still fascinating, because it aptly illustrated the polarity of views Christians have when dealing with "visible" sin. (I use the word *visible* because there are really two kinds of sins, aren't there? The covert sins that we all commit—gossip, covetousness, greed, idolatry, dishonesty, laziness—which never spark controversy, and those sins that get everyone up in arms—like an out-of-wedlock pregnancy, theft, or drug use.)

Half the staff showered Violette with hugs, words of affirmation, and money to help with Pampers and baby food. Violette's face lit up with one huge smile when she bid good morning to those who were happy to see her back. Like the prodigal, Violette had come *home*—baby and all. It was a joyous cause for celebration! Unconditional love! Half of the staff believed that this is what a community of faith should do.

But some of the staff members were not so excited. Were they backward, coldhearted, and missing the essence of their Christian faith? Some people might think so. But these same people provided meals for Violette, drove her to the doctor's office, or babysat her child during the afternoon so she could attend a GED class. They were not mean spirited or self-righteous; they were sincerely concerned for the well-being of this young woman.

ROAD MARKER

Sometimes we have to cross the road to
give a person a second chance.

But here was the rub for them: it made them uncomfortable that Violette was holding a *visible* position in the lobby. I received a number of memos in my in-box stating their concerns. For them, having an unwed teen mother answering phones might send a "double message" to the other children and teens in the program. "We love Violette," they assured me, "but we are concerned about the *message*. . . . We need to have standards. . . . Putting her in a public position negates what we're trying to teach our kids. . . . The younger kids will see her and think there are no consequences to her actions . . . that it's okay to have sex and make babies." These well-intentioned saints offered me another suggestion: "Put Violette on *probation.* Meet with her weekly for counsel and Bible study, but take her away from the front desk."

THE MESSAGE BEHIND THE MESSAGE

To put it mildly, directing ministries that include staff and volunteers who come from various theological perspectives is a challenge. Diversity is always problematic for people. But it's not unique to youth ministry organizations. Churches, Bible study groups, Sunday school classes, and small-group fellowships deal with these issues constantly. Everyone within a Christian community has an opinion or an interpretation of how situations should be handled. The question of who deserves to be "in" and who should be "out" never seems to go away. It is a consistent theme in the Gospels, a scenario that Jesus continually confronted.

As a ministry leader, I understood the tension that came to a head with Violette. As a participant in various churches and other expressions of Christian community, I understand the divisive nature of similar situations. In our ministry context, through our Bible studies, wacky skits, retreats, and discipleship groups, our workers beckon young people to higher moral and spiritual standards. Whether it's the lyrics of the music they are addicted to, the language they use when speaking to one another, or the sexual ethics of the culture in which they live, we want them to reexamine these things in light of Scripture. We want our youth to consider a new way of living, because we believe that certain behaviors are ultimately destructive.

But what happens when our kids (or friends, choir members, or deacons) fall short of the biblical standards we (or our churches) preach? What is our course of action? And more important, what message do our *actions* send to the people whom we serve? What is the real message that seeps into the subconscious of those who do not "measure up"? Not the message we *think* they hear. Not the message we *want* them to hear.

What message would people in our neighborhoods receive if Violette were fully welcomed back into our community? And what message would be received if Violette were welcomed back *with limitations* or not welcomed back at all? The distinction is important to consider. Likewise, how would we handle a similar situation in our church? in our men's group? in our women's Bible study? The way we handle certain situations sends a loud message to those on the periphery, those looking in.

Violette initially chose the isolation of a dark basement over the potentially restorative fellowship of Christian community. Her decision said a lot about how Christian communities are often perceived by people who feel they do not measure up. It was easier for her to deal with loneliness and depression than to confront the shame and embarrassment of making a mistake. Violette eventually decided that our ministry was no longer a place where she could work through her struggles. Even though no staff worker ever explicitly kicked her out, she concluded that this place was not friendly to failure. (I'm thankful that today Violette is doing well and works as a dental assistant.)

That concerned me. Not because I thought we needed to dismiss her sin. Any loving adult knows that there are social, physical, and emotional issues tied to our destructive behaviors and that those behaviors need to be avoided for our long-term health and spiritual vibrancy. Our moral standards continually need to be discussed and challenged.

But it is essential for alienated human beings to have a safe, loving, nonjudgmental place to work through their particular struggles—a place where they can talk openly and honestly about what is really happening in their lives. And if the people of Christ do not provide this forum, then where will people turn? My fear was that if our community relegated Violette to a back corner office, "punished" with weekly probationary Bible studies and counseling sessions, the message perceived by the larger population would be that our faith community was only for people who *do not mess up*.

If this became the perception in the neighborhoods, would a

ROAD MARKER

Sometimes we have to cross the road to offer
a safe haven for someone in need.

---

kid dealing with questions of sexual identity feel that our community was a safe place to voice those issues? Would a young man addicted to pornography feel safe enough to confess and seek counsel from a staff member if he knew he would be put on probation? Would the college student struggling to make sense of her belief in God be welcomed to share her doubts? Not likely.

If people—men and women with addictions, college students asking existential questions, youth finding their identity—do not feel that they can work through their issues within the context of a Christian community, where will they work through them? Nightclubs? Internet chat rooms? Philosophy classes? The local bar? If people perceive that acceptance into a Christian community is built around moral success and doctrinal certitude, then I fear that people who really need Christian community will find other places to work out their moral failings and questions.[2] Or if they do continue to show up, they will mask all their problems and lie to our faces about what is really happening in their lives.

M. Scott Peck, in his book *The Different Drum*, argues that the critical ingredient in forming true community is *vulnerability*. But he adds that vulnerability will take place only when people feel it is *safe* enough to be honest. Most groups of people (especially religious groups), contends Peck, get stuck in a kind of "pseudocommunity." We find no safety in our churches, so we play the church game. This pseudocommunity is a place where "people who want to be loving attempt to be so by telling little white lies, by withholding some of the truth about themselves and their feelings in order to avoid conflict."[3]

Wasn't that Violette's story? Obviously she had been actively engaged in sexual activity while attending our programs. The only thing that eventually pushed her out of our pseudocommunity was the fact that the truth about her could no longer be hidden—she would either need to confess or leave. She chose to leave. We must realize that our churches will never become communities if people sense that moral failure means second-class citizenship.

Abandoned and discarded people need whole, loving communities of faith. They need to taste and experience those places where they can be honest, places where they can work through their deepest struggles. As adults we must work to create these kinds of spaces, and we must make sure the "message behind the message" is not one of exclusion.

For all of us, being relationally connected to the body of Christ is a significant part of our salvation story. Alienation from honest relationships with other believers cripples our capacity to heal and discover our place in God's larger drama in the world. Therefore we must pray that our best intentions never create stumbling blocks for those needing fellowship, excluding them from the intimacy they so desperately need.

SENDING A NEW MESSAGE

Have you ever talked with people who are reluctant to enter a church or have been turned off to God because they feel they do not measure up? "Once I get myself together, then I will start attending," said one individual to me recently. "I'm just too bad to hang out with those Christian folk," claimed another. What a sad commentary on how Christ's message is perceived by those outside the community of faith.

Recently I watched a television show that highlighted a Christian group protesting the "immorality" of a particular city. There were the Christians on one side of the street, screaming in the name of God and attempting to "reclaim" the culture for

God. On the other side of the street were those "sinners," calling the Christians intolerant bigots. As the voices got louder, each group became more emboldened, more convinced of their position. Tragically, no one crossed the road.

So how do God's people send a different message? It begins by our willingness to cross roads and allow ourselves to enter into the lives of those who feel alienated, rejected, and unloved. Only when we enter that place can we begin the process of encouraging those living in the valley of dry bones and leading them across the road toward loving communities that hold forth new life.

CHAPTER SEVEN

CROSSING THE ROAD TO OUR ENEMIES

*But true courage is not to hate our enemy, any more
than to fight and kill him. To love him, to love in
the teeth of his hate—that is real bravery. That
ought to earn people m-m-medals.*

DOM JOSEPH WARRILOW[1]

One of my favorite true-story films is *Joyeux Noël*. Critics found
it sentimental but they were all unanimous in their admiration
for its director, Christian Carion.

Joyeux Noël recounts a Christmas Eve truce among German,
English, and French forces during World War I. With its hand-
to-hand combat, mustard gas, disease, and crude medical tech-
niques, historians often refer to the Great War as the most
gruesome war of the modern-day world.

The setting for the film is a three-trench triangle in the middle
of a farmer's field in northern France. Germans are in one trench,
French in another, British in a third. The British and French
were allies—though they had little regard for one another. The
German army was their common enemy. For months the soldiers
burrowed into their trenches like malnourished groundhogs, yet
they were valiant warriors who fought to hold a few feet of land,
hating and distrusting the enemy who was trying to annihilate
them. It was barbaric and savage warfare.

The drama begins on a Christmas Eve when a few Scots in
the English trench assemble their bagpipes and begin to play

Christmas carols. Nicholas Sprink, a famous tenor in Germany who has been drafted into the army, hears the music and responds to the bagpipes by singing "Silent Night" in his native tongue. As his incredible voice drifts through the chill December air, it triggers a chain of unlikely events. The Scottish bagpipes recalibrate their tune and begin accompanying Sprink across the dark field. Suddenly the Germans hoist several dozen small candlelighted trees that have been delivered to the front lines by a charitable group, placing them on the top of their trenches.

In the pitch-black night, the flickering candles can be seen for a mile. The Catholic chaplain in the English trench then bellows out "O Come, All Ye Faithful." As if on cue, the men crawl out from their trenches and gather in the middle of the grenade-pocked battlefield, stepping carefully over the dead bodies of their collective comrades.

Naturally, each move is made with suspicious caution. But then a French soldier, tentative but singing, offers a piece of chocolate to a reluctant German. The German refuses to take it. When the weary French soldier breaks off a piece for himself and places the delicious morsel in his mouth, a spirit of mutual sharing between the enemies is unleashed—liquor, cigarettes, and family photos are passed around amidst fractured languages and laughter. A few men jokingly argue about who owns a scruffy cat that wanders in and out of the various trenches begging food and attention.

What happens between those groups of soldiers is what happens when we encounter those we distrust and view as "those evil people." As the warring soldiers' eyes are opened, they begin to see that they have more in common than they could have guessed. They are husbands, fathers, and lovers. They have children whom they love deeply and miss terribly. Some have girlfriends to whom they want to return. These ordinary men have been placed in unfortunate situations. Governments and propaganda have taught them to hate the enemy. Commanding officers and drill sergeants have taught them to kill. But when the veneer of a uniform is stripped away these men are alike, human beings who would rather be home with their loved ones than launching grenades.

One of the most powerful quotes of the movie is made by French lieutenant Audebert. Audebert never actually believes in the war. "We have more in common with the German soldiers than with the French politicians that are sending us off into the war." In that faraway farmer's field of nearly a century ago, the eyes of the former enemies are opened to a new reality.

ROAD MARKER

Sometimes we have to cross the road to see
that our enemies are just like us.

My favorite character in the film is the priest, Father Palmer. Palmer seizes the moment under the celestial backdrop of a clear Christmas sky and performs Holy Communion for this newly unified band of men. Soldiers who hours before were trying to kill each other now mutually celebrate the redemptive moment of Christ . . . together. The service is especially poignant because it is conducted in Latin, a language that many of the men from Germany, England, and France understand—once again, the sacred transcends human divisions. The makeshift worship service symbolically reminds the viewer that race, geography, and political beliefs are secondary to God's gift of Jesus to humanity.

With a sparkle in his eye, Father Palmer comments after his unusual Christmas Eve mass, "The altar was like a burning fire, drawing men to it because of its warmth." After spending a lifetime delivering homilies to apathetic and despondent parishioners, the priest is given the rare glimpse of witnessing faith and hope in the most dire of human conditions. Palmer is portrayed as one who understands the essence of the gospel—that human beings are created to live in relationship with God. The Good News is not restricted by borders; nor is it exclusive to a select few. The Christ child is not simply a gift for those with the best military power or those who hold the moral high ground. Ironically, later in the film Father Palmer is reprimanded by the bishop for fraternizing with the enemy and including them in the Eucharistic celebration. He is unceremoniously sent home from the front lines—a place where he wanted to remain and minister because of the rawness and openness of the men to God's love and grace.

On that Christmas Eve in 1914 a barrier was transcended—enemies came out of their trenches and for a brief period of time discovered that their foes were not evil, heartless warriors. The world was given a glimpse that night of what happens when people cross the road and come face-to-face with their enemies.

EXCUSE ME? LOVE MY ENEMIES?

One of the toughest roads we will ever cross is the road leading straight toward our enemy—it's against our very natures. Not only does crossing require courage and humility, but the reality is that our efforts may not be reciprocated or appreciated. But it is a road that Jesus not only beckons us to, but actually commands us to cross. "Love your enemies," exhorts Jesus with stunning insight. "Do good to those who hate you" (Luke 6:27). The words provide no backdoor getaways or escape hatches. Many of us would prefer the command to be optional, like, "Once in a while, if you feel like it, you should do something nice for your enemy." Most of us would like to stay on our side of the road on this one.

When it comes to enemies, Christians are fast to shift from an experiential faith to intellectualizing. We take out our *Strong's Exhaustive Concordance of the Bible*, and we look for all the references to the words *enemy, love,* or *doing good.* We do a background study on the context of the verse—maybe even blowing the dust off our Greek lexicon to understand more fully the syntax or etymological development of the words. And if we are still looking for an excuse not to love our enemy, we employ more commentaries and the wisdom of the theologians. The conservative commentators take us down the trail of historical minutiae; the liberals balk at the very notion that Jesus even spoke the words. "Phew!" we exclaim with relief after our research, "I knew there was a way out of practicing this command!" The Danish theologian Søren Kierkegaard, who never could be accused of sugarcoating his message to the church, disclosed our fondness for watering down the poignancy of Scripture:

> Take any words in the New Testament and forget everything except pledging yourself to act accordingly. My God, you will say, if I do that my whole life will be ruined. . . . Herein lies the real place of Christian scholarship. Christian scholarship is the Church's prodigious invention to defend itself against the Bible, to ensure that we can continue to be good Christians without the Bible coming too close. . . . Dreadful it is to fall into the hands of the living God. Yes, it is even dreadful to be alone with the New Testament.[2]

I think there is value in thoughtfully and intellectually engaging the Scriptures. However, when our scholarship provides excuses for avoiding difficult practices, it has lost sight of its purpose.

The challenge of following Jesus is that he was not a "do as I say, not as I do" teacher. Church history is full of hypocrites. Each one of us can probably name preachers who have exhorted us to new heights of morality and commitment before we discovered that their own decisions and commitments fell far short of their rhetoric. Not so with Jesus. Perhaps that is why it is so difficult to refute his claims. Jesus makes preposterous (seemingly impossible) claims but then turns around and puts them into practice—showing us the way through example. So the question is, do we actually *see* Jesus loving his enemies?

Of course, some might quickly point out that Jesus had an edge on us average human beings. "Jesus probably was human . . . but not *really* human." They'd say that Jesus walked down dusty roads, but he never got a blister like the rest of us. He most likely shucked and ate ears of corn as he traveled through the fields, but you can bet he never suffered indigestion. And when his disciples disappointed him, he never really felt the pangs of discouragement. Jesus, in the minds of many Christians, is a stoic who had it easy because he ducked in and out of the human realm at will. That kind of thinking is an affront to two thousand years of orthodox Christian faith and writings that claim Jesus was *fully human*—real blisters, real indigestion, real tears, real pain, and real heartbreak. Jesus' full humanity is central to our faith. Believe me, loving enemies was just as difficult for Jesus as it is for us.

MAUNDY THURSDAY

On the day before he was betrayed, Jesus was confronted with the ultimate enemy-loving challenge. Jesus would either need to reach across the road to someone who had violated Jesus' trust for his own selfish interests, or turn his back on this betrayer and his coconspirators and abandon them. According to John 13, Jesus was aware that he would be betrayed and that the betrayal would come from within his own camp—not from a Roman spy or an overly zealous Pharisee. Betrayal would come from a good friend he had trusted and with whom he had shared his life. Betrayal would come from one who had seen his miracles and listened to his teachings: a person who had never once seen him slip up. And it wasn't just the betrayer whose future actions Jesus was aware of. He knew that his closest friends later would deny any knowledge of him (Jesus? Never heard of him.), allowing him to be mocked and beaten and killed. If I'm truthful with myself, I would probably have joined that group of cowards if I had been there.

The Catholic scholar Richard John Neuhaus captures Jesus' radical act of enemy love when he explains the significance of Maundy Thursday.

> Maundy Thursday is so called because that night, the night before he was betrayed, Jesus gave the command, the *mandatum*, that we should love one another. Not necessarily with the love of our desiring, but with a demanding love, even a demeaning love—as in washing the feet of faithless friends who will run away and leave you naked to your enemies.[3]

Neuhaus reminds us that Jesus engaged in an act of love that few people would choose to exercise. If we knew that a "friend" was about to betray us, would we reach out in that kind of humility and love? If we knew our closest friends were going to flee from us during our hour of need, would we have the fortitude to hold their dirty feet in our hands hours earlier, look into their eyes, and still love them? This is the lesson that most foot-washing services forget to teach. Jesus was not simply engaging in an act of servant leadership; he was ritually cleaning the feet of a group of selfish cowards.

ROAD MARKER

Jesus crossed the road to let his enemies know that he loved them.

The mandatum is no mere abstraction. The mandatum is a call to each of us to engage in real acts of love toward those we have relegated for our own emotional and psychological protection to the other side of the road. To move in the direction of our enemies with open arms and with a spirit of service is a kind of love that cuts against the grain of our human tendencies. It is a demanding, demeaning love that becomes a transforming moment.

But Jesus' behavior and teaching still beg the question: Why cross the road to our enemies? Why extend time, resources, and emotion to those who intentionally seek to destroy or undermine our very existence? A pragmatist laughs at the lunacy of the effort. A psychologist cautions against wasting valuable emotional capital. A life coach advises against the possible career implications of such a choice. But Jesus is not a pragmatist or a psychologist or a life coach. Jesus has a larger vision for humanity—a vision bigger than our individual rights and personal careers.

It is a vision that was captured briefly on the battlefield that Christmas Eve in 1914 when enemies discovered that their perceptions and convictions about each other were wrong. The same is true when God's people initiate radical acts of love toward their enemies; the vision of Jesus is ushered into the earthly realm of existence . . . even if just for a moment.

WHAT'S IN IT FOR ME?

What's the benefit? Will I really grow in faith? Will my enemy really change?

Here is the sobering truth: there is no guarantee of *any* benefit, no promise of happily ever after, no immediate payoff for our obedience. Loving our enemies is wrought with all kinds of disastrous possibilities—both physically and emotionally. Church history is laden with examples of faithful followers who reached out in love to their enemies and, in return, lost their lives, spent years in jail, or were separated from their loved ones. There was a cost to their obedience. There was pain and suffering involved.

Then why do it?

First, *Jesus clearly and frequently instructs us to do so.* "Love your enemies, do good to those who hate you" (Luke 6:27). In faith we engage in this kind of love because it calls us to trust God for the outcome. From a human perspective, loving the enemy does not make sense. And in the film, to those bishops and military officials who heard about their soldiers celebrating the Eucharist with the opposing army, it was completely absurd—suicidal lunacy, nonsensical. But from a divine perspective, in so doing we open one more door for God to initiate a movement of the miraculous in our personal lives and in our world.

The late Henri Nouwen captures another reason for followers of Christ to engage in this radical practice of enemy love. Nouwen writes:

> Whenever, contrary to the world's vindictiveness, we love our enemy, we exhibit something of the perfect love of God, whose will is to bring all human beings together as children of one Father. Whenever we forgive instead of letting fly at one another, bless instead of cursing one another, tend one another's wounds instead of rubbing salt into them, hearten instead of discouraging one another, give hope instead of driving one another to despair, hug instead of harassing one another, welcome instead of coldshouldering one another, thank instead of criticizing one another, praise instead of maligning one another . . . in short, whenever we opt for and not against one another, we make God's unconditional love visible; we are diminishing violence and giving birth to a new community."[4]

Nouwen highlights two important truths. First, by exercising this counterintuitive love toward those who have hurt us and those we despise, we have the sacred opportunity of making "God's unconditional love visible." In a world skeptical and jaded by God-talking pundits, making visible the perfect love of God is a chance for the world to see authentic faith in its purest form.

Nouwen also underscores the possibility of aiding in the birth of a new human community—a community governed by love and forgiveness, not hatred and revenge. Some may call this pie-in-the-sky dreaming, but there are historical examples of people and communities who chose to forgive their enemies, rather than seek revenge. The Amish in Pennsylvania delivered food and money to the wife of the man who murdered their children in the schoolhouse massacre in October 2006; blacks in South Africa forgave their white Afrikaner oppressors through the Truth and Reconciliation Commission formed after the abolition of apartheid; Rwandan Tutsi forgave Hutu who slaughtered their families in one of the worst genocides in modern history. These are examples of the Christian community laying the foundation for a new kind of world. These expressions of hope all began with a willingness to cross the road.

THE PROBLEM OF SHERMAN

I did not like Sherman the instant I met him. That's not good for a youth worker who loves young people and whose purpose is to point them to God.

Sherman was an oversize—make that tall and meaty—thirteen-year-old with an aggressively big, bad attitude to match.

Unfortunately, Sherman occasionally attended our youth programs at church and frequently interrupted my classroom activities. Not long into my life's work, I discovered that there were multiple quirky children who could push my buttons. I could live with the mischievous but likable delinquents; a burp or two in the middle of the Lord's Prayer or a reworking of the lyrics to "Amazing Grace" (don't ask) isn't malicious. But then there were the kids who were purposefully mean and hurtful. Sherman was the leader of that camp.

On this particular day Sherman caught me off guard.

I had just buckled the first eight children into the church's fifteen-passenger van (I was a lone worker) and had returned to the church basement for the remaining seven. It would take me twenty-seven minutes to drop off the second- and third-grade class—up Westfield Avenue, right on Thirty-Second, left on Beideman Avenue—and then I would come back to the church for the fourth through sixth graders. It was a well-timed routine that I drove each Monday through Friday at 5:45 P.M.

When I emerged from the basement with my second string of little ones, I noticed a large body in the van. Sherman! As I got a little closer I heard the children screaming. Sherman was hitting some of them. I yelled something inappropriate for a minister to say.

I was outraged! Jumping into the van, I grabbed Sherman by his belt and yanked him into the parking lot. He staggered as his feet landed on the asphalt.

"Don't you touch me, man! Or I'll bust you up!"

"Kids, get in the van. Now." In a flash, they complied.

"Come on, man." Sherman raised his fists ready to spar. "Come on, hit me, you coward. I dare you."

At that moment I wished I hadn't been a Christian. I have a great right hook and wanted in the worst way to use it. But with fifteen impressionable children with noses pressed against the windows, watching their *minister*, I didn't think it would be the best witness of God's forgiving love to engage in that kind of righteous anger, i.e., violence.

But I did something almost as bad.

Sherman was wearing a brand-new North Carolina State baseball cap. As he danced and swerved around me, I reached out and with one impressive move, flicked it off his head. Sherman erupted into a hysterical fit of rage. When he quickly bent to pick the treasured hat off the pavement, I took advantage of the opening, ran around the van to the driver's side, jumped in, rolled up the window, and turned the key. The weary engine jumped into action and we were gone.

As I sped out of the parking lot, an enraged thirteen-year-old ran beside me, pounding on the window. With my composure back, I floored the bus down Westfield Avenue. Aha, I had gotten the upper hand, the last lick, without violating too many Christian principles. I smiled smugly. *I showed that kid.*

A GIFT OF CHOCOLATES

When I got home that night I shared the day's events with my wife, Pam. To my surprise, Pam didn't take my side. Instead, she gently reminded me that Sherman was a kid and I was the adult. "Why don't you reach out to that kid and make a peace offering." *Was she out of her mind?* After I had calmed down, Pam said she had a box of wrapped chocolates on the dining room table. "Bruce, why don't you walk down the street and give them to Sherman?"

The last thing I ever wanted to do was give that kid a gift and apologize for how I had handled the situation. After all, I was justified in my behavior. He deserved the treatment he'd received.

The chocolates sat on the table. Two days. A week. Two weeks.

"Are you going to take the chocolates?" Pam prodded me one day.

As far as I was concerned I had compartmentalized the event to one of the darker parts of my cerebral cortex. Sherman hadn't shown his face at church since the incident. Delivering a peace offering would only stir up old memories and potential conflict. Why take a chance? I would just avoid him. If he showed up on the church campus I would call the police and have him escorted off the property.

But deep down in my gut I knew Pam was right. There was something wrong in my universe, and I had the opportunity to correct it.

Several days later, as I was retrieving my garbage cans from the end of the driveway, I spied Sherman at the end of the block. Walking back into the house I saw the wrapped box of chocolates and knew this was my moment—it was now or never! I grabbed the box from the house and headed down the street.

When I was within a hundred yards of Sherman he caught sight of me. Rather than retreating he began to walk aggressively toward me, obviously not intimidated by someone three times his age. I kept thinking to myself, *When I was his age I would have run as fast as possible from an approaching adult.* But Sherman was two inches taller than I and outweighed me by several pounds; I was no threat. In his brief life, he had chased down more formidable foes than me.

"I brought you a box of chocolates," I said when he got within ten feet. I extended the little package in the palm of my hand. Sherman stopped dead in his tracks and stared blankly at me. Startled, he eyed the package.

"Go on. Take it. It's a peace offering."

Sherman took the package, held it at arm's length, and awkwardly began to untie the ribbon with his free hand, slowly, as though he were a bomb squad officer expecting the box to explode.

When he lifted the box top and saw the individually wrapped chocolates in gold foil, he looked at me for a long moment. He grunted, "Thanks," turned, and disappeared down the street.

The next day, I was standing in the church parking lot about to climb into the red fifteen-passenger van to do my midday errands—a mail drop at the post office, a fill-up at Texaco, and a stop at Save-A-Lot for cookies for the kids in our after-school program.

From the corner of the parking lot, I spied Sherman. He stopped a couple of feet from the van and stared at me.

"Do you want a ride?" I asked, trying to break the ice. I motioned him around to the passenger side.

For the next two hours Sherman and I ran errands together. We exchanged a few words about the Philadelphia Phillies and the upcoming Eagles season, but I never managed to get the conversation around to why he was so angry, why he felt it necessary to be such a pest. (Don't say what you're thinking.) But we did spend time together.

For the next few years, Sherman drifted in and out of our programs. We never became best friends, but he never did anything harmful or malicious again.

ROAD MARKER

Sometimes we have to cross the road and deliver
a peace offering of chocolate.

I did learn the obvious about him: Sherman was a struggling, troubled adolescent, trying to make some sense of his raging hormones, a fatherless home, a violent and poverty-filled neighborhood. Beneath his tough, arrogant exterior was just a very young boy in a man's body—a boy who did not need another enemy. He needed to experience a different kind of behavior from the adults in his life.

I wish I could say that Sherman went on to become a minister or a significant role model for younger inner-city children. I wish I could say that the definitive moment in Sherman's life was getting those chocolates from a reluctant youth leader. Unfortunately I do not know what happened to Sherman. I lost contact. I hope he is doing some great things.

But I can tell you what happened to me when I carried my peace offering down Thirty-Seventh Street many years ago. That afternoon was when I first saw the power of "enemy love" at work. I was given the opportunity to see what can happen when we put the seemingly impossible teachings of Jesus into practice.

Was global conflict abated that afternoon by my actions in an obscure East Camden neighborhood? No. Was the Middle East crisis resolved by my actions? Absolutely not. The world moved on that afternoon—births and deaths, genocide and tremendous humanitarian acts of relief. There were acts of evil and there were acts of sacrificial love. But in my life, in a very small way, I was reminded that an enemy is just another human being, a human being with fears, feelings, hurts, and insecurities. And that, as a follower of Christ, I am called to meet those human beings and attempt as best I can to show love.

In a letter, Trappist monk and writer Thomas Merton reminded his friend Dorothy Day, an advocate for the poorest of the poor in New York City, that our job as Christians is to love others without stopping to inquire whether or not they are worthy. That is not our business. What we are asked to do is to love, and this love will render both ourselves and our neighbors worthy, if anything can. Merton's challenge to his friend is our challenge as we seek to embody the heart of God through loving our enemies.

My friend Michael Doyle, an edgy Irish priest who has ministered in our city for thirty-five years, puts it this way: "The greatest compliment Jesus ever gave a human being was the command to love our enemies. Why? Because Jesus believed humans had the capacity and kindness to exercise such a difficult and counterintuitive act." What a wonderful perspective on this command. Let's embrace this amazing compliment and unearth our ability to do the difficult thing. Jesus believes we can.

CHAPTER EIGHT

CROSSING THE ROAD OF CULTURAL WORLDVIEW

Lord, don't trouble yourself, for I do not deserve to have you come under my roof.

LUKE 7:6

From my office to the Half Moon coffee shop is a mere twelve blocks down Maple Avenue. With the posted speed limit 25 miles per hour, the trip there is agonizingly slow and requires absolute discipline of my right foot. I believe Maple Avenue is the most patrolled road in America, a cash cow for the local police.

Those vigilant officers especially fancied my '77 Chevy Nova, which I drove for ten years. They would wait in the shadows of the off-ramp watching for "suspicious" cars entering their community. The fact that I was driving from the inner city into the suburbs placed my ugly twenty-two-year-old Nova at the top of the local patrol car's most wanted list. Routinely, I was pulled over and questioned: a broken taillight, crooked license plate, failure to put on a blinker. Any trivial offense and they pulled me over, displaying their authority to its full effect—flashing lights, sirens, and the megaphoned voice demanding that the "golden Nova" pull over.

My most memorable event was being pulled over after our annual fund-raising banquet. After an insanely long day and a glorious evening of raising money for youth in our community, I saw the flashing lights trailing me. After what I thought was an empathy-invoking story, the officer still gave me a $28 ticket for a burned-out taillight. Needless to say it put a damper on the evening. Consequently, over the years I became more than a little paranoid; I became a rearview-mirror looker, always checking behind me to see if I was being followed.

That feeling made me wonder what it must have been like for the Jews in Nazi concentration camps or the Russians banished to the gulags. For them, any minor infraction, real or supposed, brought horrible retribution. Fortunately, most of us do not live in an environment where we are constantly watched and threatened with severe consequences when we step out of line. But this is not the case for many people in the world.

And it wasn't the case for Jesus when he walked the dusty roads of Galilee.

LIVING UNDER AN OCCUPYING FORCE

During Jesus' life and ministry, Israel was occupied territory ruled by a foreign force. The Roman military cruelly controlled what the nationals did. Jewish political leaders were mere puppets of the empire, and Temple priests were co-opted by Rome to keep the masses calm. For example, if a Roman soldier asked a Jew to carry his equipment, the Jewish citizen was required by law to carry it a mile (Matthew 5:41). These were sixty- to eighty-pound bags—not counting weapons! There are historical records of whole villages fleeing at the sight of approaching soldiers, just to avoid being conscripted or having their animals seized. There was definitely no love lost between the two sides. Any Jewish tax collector who worked for Rome was despised and hated, for every Jew knew that his hard-earned tax money was sent to Rome to finance the emperor's affairs. Then, too, subversive Jews who challenged the system of Roman imperial rule were subject to the most brutal form of execution: they were hung on a cross. Citizens understood the consequences of stepping out of line.

JESUS STANDS UP FOR GOD

In Matthew 8:5-8 we see another poignant example of Jesus' road-crossing commitment.

> When he entered Capernaum, a centurion came to him, appealing to him and saying, "Lord, my servant is lying at home paralysed, in terrible distress." And he said to him, "I will come and cure him." The centurion answered, "Lord, I am not worthy to have you come under my roof; but only speak the word, and my servant will be healed." (NRSV)

Here Jesus crossed the road of *cultural worldview and political ideology*. The Roman soldier's belief system entirely contradicted the teachings of Jesus and the worldview of most Jews. Rome, the most powerful, oppressive, and violent empire in the ancient world for the five centuries prior to Jesus' day, was a movement rooted not only in military force, but in a kind of imperial ideology that validated their conquests.

The contrasts to Jesus' teachings are striking. He taught that for Jews there was one God—the God of Abraham, Isaac, and Jacob; Romans taught that the emperor was the son of god, the savior and redeemer, the lord of all—not an ordinary king.

Jesus believed that the land Israel possessed belonged to the Jews; Rome believed it was theirs. Jesus said that the meek will inherit the earth; the last will be first; if you are slapped on the right cheek, you must offer the other as well. Rome taught that might makes right, that only the strong prevail, and that using military force and violence is the best way to treat an enemy. Rome's marching orders were peace by whatever means needed. Jesus' marching orders were peace through love.

The two belief systems could not have been more at odds. And yet Jesus and his followers, along with the people Jesus was encountering, walked the same streets, drank the same water, and breathed in the same dust as the Roman soldiers. There were definite barriers between them—barriers of different worldviews and political orientations, fortified with intense anger and resentment.

And yet, for most of the Roman occupation, Jews were permitted to worship and maintain their faith. It was a matter of money. The authorities realized that a peaceful and productive Israel meant Rome would need fewer soldiers on its streets and could relegate more soldiers to those warring corners of the empire. If Israel was functioning well, the Romans could send money back to Caesar's coffers and everybody would be happy. Allowing a little monotheistic worship was a small concession for potentially bigger financial dividends. So a person's religious faith was not a threat to those in power . . . unless believers challenged the system. Only then would it become a problem.

WDJD: WHAT DID JESUS DO?

When approached by the Roman centurion Jesus confronted an interesting choice. Jesus had to choose whether he was going to respond to the request of a person who personified and symbolized everything Jesus' people detested. A bystander in the crowd might think Jesus was a sympathizer of the Roman occupying forces if he responded to the soldier's request.

Entering a centurion's home also violated Jewish law that said entering the home of a Gentile was forbidden. In the eyes of the zealous religious sects, if Jesus agreed to go with the soldier he would be breaking Jewish law and selling out to the Romans; he would be considered wishy-washy in his own beliefs—someone who was theologically suspect or doctrinally weak. That type of road crossing could have undermined Jesus' ministry or made him guilty by association.

It wasn't the first incident where Jesus was under suspicion because of his choice of companions. "Why does your teacher eat with tax collectors and 'sinners'?" gossiped Jesus' critics (Matthew 9:11;

Mark 2:16; Luke 5:30). Was he really guilty of a crime because he had a crust of bread and perhaps a swallow of wine with people whom the religious establishment refused to share anything with? Endearing terms like "glutton" and "drunkard" (Matthew 11:19) followed Jesus to the cross. So crossing the road to visit a Roman soldier was additional ammunition for his critics.

Fast-forward to today and we haven't learned our lesson. This same kind of slandering happens in the Christian community more often than it should. If I am a "conservative" Christian and attend a service where a "liberal" is speaking, then I have sold out to the conservative cause. If I am a "liberal," break rank, and embrace an issue deemed "conservative," then I am ridiculed by those on the left. If I hang out with questionable people, my integrity and character is questioned. Many Christians are quick to make damaging judgments if anyone chooses to cross our socially created boundaries.

Oscar Romero, the late archbishop of El Salvador, captures this spirit of judgment when he says: "When I feed the poor, they call me a saint. When I question why people are poor, they call me a communist." His compassionate spirit remains unchanged in both circumstances.

When I think of Jesus helping a Roman soldier, I think of my Christian friends who are vehement antiwar pacifists. Out of their deep convictions and understanding of the Scriptures, they choose to protest violence in every form. They head to Washington to pray on the steps of Congress; they picket and protest missile defense manufacturers. I admire my friends who have those deep convictions and the courage to show them.

On the other hand, I also think of other Christian friends who believe that violence is sometimes necessary to suppress evil. Seldom do these two groups roast marshmallows together or hold hands during a moving rendition of "Kum Ba Yah." You probably would be hard pressed to find them at a similar worship service. Both are passionate about their convictions. To show any interest or willingness to understand the other group's position certainly would demonstrate weakness.

Jesus chose to cross the road. Not on the basis of what others would think, but rather on what he knew to be right. "I will come and cure him," records Matthew (8:7, NRSV). The consequences of Jesus' road-crossing decision were twofold. First, the soldier's servant was healed. Second, Jesus made one of the most surprising statements in the Gospels. "Truly I tell you, in no one in Israel have I found such faith" (8:10, NRSV). Can you imagine the gasps in the crowd? Jesus upheld the pagan enemy—the violent oppressor—as an example of *faith*!

ROAD MARKER

Jesus crossed the road to meet a person whose faith was genuine.

Jesus' statement begs the question: what did he see in the guard that represented such an example of faith? It is evident that the man understood authority and how authoritative systems worked. He acknowledged Jesus' authority and his ability to make his servant well.

> "For I also am a man under authority, with soldiers under me; and I say to one, 'Go,' and he goes, and to another, 'Come,' and he comes, and to my slave, 'Do this,' and the slave does it." When Jesus heard him, he was amazed and said to those who followed him, "Truly I tell you, in no one in Israel have I found such faith."
> (Matthew 8:9-10, NRSV)

Something about the centurion's response unequivocally grabbed Jesus' attention, compelling Jesus to single him out as a premier model of active faith. Was it the soldier's certainty of Jesus' ability to heal? Was it his compassionate heart and concern for his servant? Was it his humility? Biblical scholars continue to debate the point.

There is an important secondary message that Matthew is underscoring with this story. Matthew intentionally includes the centurion's encounter with Jesus in his Gospel because of how it upset and dismayed those who heard it. Talk about more than a few bruised egos and a lot of fodder for juicy gossip! I can imagine them mumbling, "Preposterous!" "Where does Jesus get off proclaiming that the man with the greatest faith in Israel is a man who isn't even a Jew?"

It would be the equivalent in our day of Nelson Mandela pointing to a white Afrikaner as a model of compassion during the height of apartheid, or Martin Luther King Jr. upholding one of Bull Connor's policemen in Selma as the embodiment of love, or Gandhi using a British soldier as a metaphor for self-restraint. Come on, Jesus, don't you know your audience? Fortunately for us, Jesus never backpedaled on the truth.

Jesus crossed roads to remind people that our best spiritual lessons are often discovered in places that we never imagined. Disorienting dilemmas open us up to truth in extraordinary ways. Encounters with enemies, or people of a different race, or brothers and sisters of different socioeconomic status, or neighbors who hold different political positions can become rich reservoirs for our discovery of spiritual truth—truth that can change us. It is on the other side of the road that Jesus encountered this rare expression of faith, an expression that Jesus still wants us to embrace in our lives.

LEARNING FROM A SUFI

My friend John attends a conservative Bible church that regularly preaches contempt for Muslims—especially in the aftermath of 9/11. Sitting in the pew one Sunday morning, John

decided it was time to do a little research on the people his
pastor so virulently derided. John is smart, has a university
education, works in finances. In his business life he spends his
day scrutinizing investments and company spreadsheets; why
wouldn't he do the same intensive research about Muslims? The
only thing he knew about Muslims was what he had heard from
his pastor and what he read in the papers. He had never really
met nor talked to a Muslim.

So John joined an interfaith group. There were weekly meetings
at the local university. John started attending the gathering, where
Muslims, Jews, Buddhists, and Christians came together to discuss
current affairs, faith, and politics. Initially John was a little skeptical and nervous, but he soon found the discussions stimulating
and informative. He still believed in his Christian convictions and
shared them forthrightly, but he discovered that there were other
people in the world who were sincere in their faith and engaged in
matters that tried to improve the quality of life for all humanity.

When his pastor discovered that John was attending those
meetings, he was livid. The very notion that John would sit down
with Muslims in an effort to understand what they thought was
apostasy. "Why would you want to talk to those people?" reprimanded the pastor. "You know they don't believe Jesus is the Son
of God. Don't you know that their religion is violent?"

Some of John's fellow parishioners—old friends, he thought—
were informed about what he was doing and joined the pastor's
critical bandwagon. Suddenly, John began receiving nasty e-mails
and notes and was confronted verbally at church. But John didn't
react by leaving his church. He and his wife had gone there for
years, and both of them had wonderful lasting memories of the
role the church had played in their lives.

At the interfaith gathering John met a Sufi woman. Sufism
is a mystical sect within the Muslim religion. Many Sufis have
roots in Iran and have set aside the literal words of Muhammad

for what one might call spiritual interpretations. Dreams, visions, music, and worship are all part of the Sufi experience.

"Would you like to join us Saturday for our special gathering?" she asked. "A Sufi master is in town, and I would like you to meet him."

"Sure. It would be an honor."

When John arrived at the gathering, about sixty people were there in the room. "I was the only non-Muslim and stuck out like a sore thumb. Everyone sat on the floor, men on one side; women on the other. We had taken off our shoes at the door. Our host whispered something into the ear of the master, and I was ceremoniously led to the chair next to him. That felt really awkward. Everybody was on the floor, and all of a sudden, I'm in the chair of honor.

"Throughout the master's talk, he asked my opinion on a number of issues—he knew I was a Christian, but that didn't seem to bother him." John paused for a moment. "What really interested me was the content of his talk. He exhorted his fellow Muslims to take back their faith from the radical extremists, reminding the people that true faith is about love.

"When the service was over everybody in the room came and gave me hugs and greetings. They thanked me for coming, even asked me to come back. I tell you, I felt more love, more hospitality in that room than I have in many churches. It just blew me away."

John was surprised by his experience with his Sufi friends. He is still a Christian, still follows Jesus each day, and still loves to sing "How Great Thou Art." But the experience with the Sufis changed his view of Muslims and continues to personally challenge him to grow in biblical faith and love.

ROAD MARKER

Sometimes we have to cross the road and listen
to another person's experience with faith.

"Do you know the only person in the Koran who has the attributes of divinity?" John asked me as he finished his story. I shook my head, revealing my own ignorance. "Jesus!" He smiled at his newfound knowledge. "How about why Muslims pray five times a day?" Again, I stared at him blankly. "Because the Christians with whom Muhammad was in contact prayed six times a day, every four hours. Muhammad didn't feel it necessary to do the midnight shift." *I have some things to learn too.*

If Jesus had been at that Sufi worship service, he might have whispered to John, "I have not found such 'love' in all the churches I have attended." In the story of the centurion, Jesus lifted up the Roman's faith so his followers would not become smug and comfortable, thinking that as God's chosen people they had the edge on such matters.

Sometimes we find incredible expressions of faith in the strangest places. That Saturday afternoon in a room full of Sufi Muslims, my friend John's eyes were opened to the reality that there are people outside of his community who are passionately devoted to following God and truly welcoming strangers. The words of the apostle John remind us of the universality of love: "Beloved, let us love one another, for love is from God; and everyone who loves is born of God and knows God" (1 John 4:7-8, NASB).

REDEMPTION IN DIRTY POLITICS

If you had met Lee Atwater in 1988 you would have found yourself in the presence of an aggressive, cocky campaign manager who would stop at nothing to get his man—George H. W. Bush—elected. He was known as the bad boy of politics whose main objective was to beat Bush's Democratic opponent, Michael Dukakis.

Atwater's strategy came straight from Taoist ideas found in *The Art of War*, a book of military strategy written in the sixth century BC by Chinese military commander Sun Tzu. One of Sun Tzu's main strategies was "Know your enemy." So Atwater went to work, discovering the weaknesses and vulnerabilities of his opponent. The word *mercy* was not in Atwater's vocabulary. A presidency was on the line; a career and reputation were at stake; a future nomination as chair of the Republican National Committee would be his reward. So he pulled out all the mean-spirited, vitriolic stops.

Atwater used the media like a magician uses a deck of cards, particularly exploiting a black murderer, Willie Horton, in politically damaging TV ads. Horton had raped a white woman after he had escaped while on furlough from a Massachusetts prison. The overzealous Republican strategist made Horton a "running mate" of Dukakis.[1] After all, it was Dukakis's legislation that had allowed this murderer back on the streets. The TV ads worked brilliantly, fully playing to the American people's subconscious fears and racial stereotypes. Dukakis's career was decimated.

A few years after becoming the toast of Washington, Atwater was diagnosed with terminal brain cancer. In 1991 he apologized for what he had done to Dukakis and other Democratic "enemies."[2] In an extended interview in *Life* magazine, Atwater explained his dramatic turnaround.

> Long before I was struck with cancer, I felt something stirring in American society. It was a sense among the people of the country—Republicans and Democrats alike—that something was missing from their lives, something crucial. I was trying to position the Republican Party to take advantage of it. But I wasn't exactly sure what "it" was. My illness helped me to see that what was missing in society is what was missing in me: a little heart, a lot of brotherhood.[3]

Atwater then called for the leaders of the nineties to "speak to this spiritual vacuum at the heart of American society, this tumor of the soul."[4]

ROAD MARKER

Sometimes we have to cross the road and ask
forgiveness before it's too late.

It is interesting how imminent death causes people to reflect on their lives in ways that surprise everyone. Atwater's confession shocked his Washington friends. Even Dukakis was surprised . . . and grateful. But death also has a way of dissolving barriers that divide people. When confronted with our mortality we begin to see the futility and pettiness of our differences. We are reminded in death that we are more similar than different.

On his deathbed Atwater realized that the categories of Republican and Democrat were really irrelevant against the backdrop of "it"—a spiritual vacuum that could not be filled by charismatic politicians or partisan policies. Atwater's confession helps us to realize that if we can cross roads of politics, religion, and ideology, we might be surprised to find human beings on the other side with whom we can work and begin to solve humanity's deeper issues . . . as brothers and sisters.

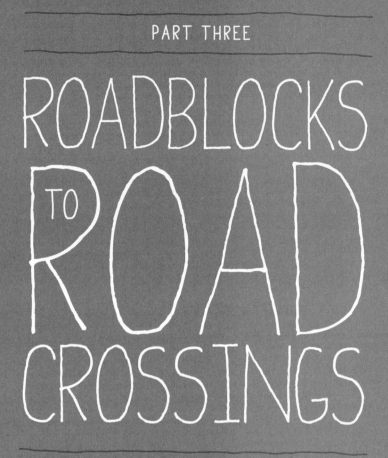

PART THREE

ROADBLOCKS TO ROAD CROSSINGS

CHAPTER NINE

THE ROADBLOCK OF FEAR

*Irrational fear is running amok, and
often with tragic results.*

DANIEL GARDNER, *THE SCIENCE OF FEAR*

"What do you think of when you hear the words *inner city*?"
I asked a wealthy congregation that was about twenty miles outside one of America's poorest cities. After a moment of silence, a
hand was tentatively raised at the back of the room.

"Frightening," exclaimed a handsomely dressed middle-aged
woman who was now standing.

"Frightening?" I asked.

"Well," she stammered, "people out here where we live are
afraid. We're afraid to go into the scary city. I would never go."

I appreciated her honesty. She had articulated the feelings
and thoughts of the silent majority. I was about to ask the audience another question when suddenly a gentleman on my right
blurted out, "Destruction! Everything in the city is in a state of
decay. Buildings are abandoned. Buildings are falling down. The
city should be bulldozed. Blown up, then rebuilt."

I was caught a little off guard by his vehemence. He was direct
and angry, but I knew where he was coming from. As a hardworking suburban businessman, his taxes underwrite 75 percent of the
city's operating budget. Deeply frustrated, suburbanites feel that
inner-city ghettos get funding and more funding, but nothing

109

ever seems to change. The city operates with corrupt city officials, poor educational systems, and crumbling infrastructures.

Yet despite the obvious problems and perception, the city
is home for thousands of people—a place of family roots and
memories. It is a place where parents and grandparents raise their
children. They're frustrated with what happens in the city too,
but they still have to go about their daily business and try to
make the best of life. A poor, dangerous neighborhood looks
different from the inside.

What suburbanites know about these communities is what
the media deems newsworthy—and, unfortunately, that often
is negative. Are the fears justifiable, legitimate? They can be.
In Camden, cars get stolen, drugs are sold, people get killed.
It's normal to be afraid of places where there is a higher probability of getting hurt. Fear is part of the human condition, a
natural response when our lives are threatened or our identities
challenged.

But fear is not the whole problem. The problem is the influ-
ence fear has to change us.

THE INSIDIOUS POWER OF FEAR

Fear can, and often does, control our actions, our thoughts, our
faith. Fear can dictate where we live and where we worship. From
my perspective, fear too frequently is the barrier that keeps us
from stepping beyond the familiar and into the realm of the
uncertain. It is that internal mechanism that clicks on and off,
telling us where to *run to* and what to *run from*. We all have the
switch. It is part of our biological and psychological makeup that
triggers our deepest human need to survive.

But there is hope. Joseph Nye says in his book *The Powers to
Lead* that "the amygdala region of human brains that regulates
fear and aggression is hardwired to react to strangers, but people
can be trained to accept diversity so that their amygdala does
not activate fight-or-flight responses when exposed to strangers."[1]

Part of the challenge of being a Christian is to acknowledge our most primitive human response to people different from ourselves. Rather than condemning ourselves for these feelings of fear—which are part of our biological makeup—we have the opportunity of transforming fear into friendship by resisting the temptation to objectify the other person and flee.

The core of the Christian faith reminds us that self-preservation is not our highest calling, especially since one of the most common phrases in the Bible is "fear not" (over 350 times!). Jesus told his followers that to save one's life is really to lose it, and to lose one's life is really to gain it. If there is a consistent message from Jesus to his followers, it is that we are called to "die" to our deepest human needs. Our life is not our own, and God will be with us wherever we go.

It's simple in theory but extremely difficult in application. However, if we are going to be active road crossers we must confront this roadblock called fear. We must acknowledge its presence, request God's help to address it head-on, and then grow through it. If we do not rise to this challenge, our potential for growth will be significantly stunted and God's movement in the world will be diminished.

CONFRONT THE PLACE WE MOST FEAR

"Go to hell."

It was a memorable opening line; I wish I had been there to witness it myself.

The setting was the chapel service at the Presbyterian Seminary in Louisville, Kentucky. That morning, Dr. Hal Warheim, professor of Christianity and Society, a prepossessing, white-haired gentleman, stood up and uttered those words to an auditorium packed with seminarians, administrators, and professors.

If I close my eyes, I can see the looks of shock on their faces: the seminary president in the front row sitting next to a VIP donor who was, after the guest speaker, supposed to make the lead donation for the school's $15 million capital campaign; the progressive seminarian awakened from her usual chapel nap looking like she'd just drunk three espressos; behind the organ, the worship leader bewildered, wondering what hymn—"Fairest Lord Jesus"?—might enhance the morning message.

The Bible passage Professor Warheim preached from that morning was Exodus 3. I realize this is a book about Jesus (and we'll come back to how Jesus dealt with fear), but there are tremendous parallels between Jesus' and Moses' stories. Both men were human. Both men had to confront their own fears of "going to hell" in order to faithfully respond to God's call on their lives. We can draw insight and strength from the larger biblical tradition to learn how we best deal with this human condition. So back to Moses.

"I have heard the afflictions of my people," said the Lord to Moses. "I will send you to Pharaoh, that you may bring forth my people." Moses' first call as the Israelites' novice leader was to step into what was at that time the most dangerous place in the world: a place where power was abused and inhuman social policies ran rampant, a place diametrically opposed to the life-giving attributes of the Creator of the universe. And yet God asked Moses to cross the road and go to hell.

Why? Because the power structure that was bringing death and misery to God's people needed to be challenged and confronted, and Moses was the one to carry that message. From the biblical record, we know that Moses was a man of faith but his response to this road crossing suggests that he was more than a little frightened.

"Who am I, that I should go to Pharaoh and bring the Israelites out of Egypt?" (Exodus 3:11). Perhaps Moses was really thinking, *Why should I go to hell?* After all, who really wants to go to hell? Most people would look for a way out of that assignment. And Moses was certainly no exception.

ROAD MARKER

Moses crossed the road to hell, armed with a heavenly promise.

Professor Warheim's point that morning was that God needs people to go to the hellish places on earth with a message of hope and liberation. God chooses people—flawed, fearful people—to stand against insurmountable obstacles and daunting odds. If Moses was a betting man, he knew that confronting Pharaoh and hoping for a positive response was more than a long shot. And yet we all know the end of the story.

Moses walked into Egypt's hell and walked out with God's people. Evil was confronted. Evil was checked. Evil was reminded that it is not the ultimate universal power. God's people were given back their lives and given a new chance to become the people God intended them to become.

MAKING IT PERSONAL

As a young pastor, Warheim took a road that led to a mining community in western Kentucky. Not a plum appointment for a young pastor, but God had called him there. What he found was horrifying—people living hand to mouth, miners doing backbreaking labor for little money, working conditions that were inhumane, and the prevalence of deadly black-lung disease among the miners. Living conditions were equally deplorable as people scraped together what food they could and washed their laundry in polluted rivers. It was a hell on earth. Yet in the midst of this the young preacher became a voice for justice, a source of provision, the embodiment of hope—providing food, advocating for workers' rights, securing medical services.

Later in his ministry Warheim was called to a tenement in New York City where the sense of hopelessness and despair seemed overwhelming. Destitute people lived in the shadows of Wall Street; children played in drug-infested neighborhoods; slum landlords stole rents and did nothing to improve living conditions. Again, Warheim put actions behind his words by fighting for improved living conditions, feeding families, and creating ministries for children.

The role of the church is to free people from all the "pharaohs" of the world, people who are responsible for conditions that make it nearly impossible for others to hope and grow spiritually. "Go to those little hells," Warheim charged his audience. "To those places where evil is the strongest and human need is the greatest; set people free to experience and serve the living God."

"Go to hell," says God. "And I will go with you."

IS "GOING TO HELL" A BIBLICAL MESSAGE?

I have heard a generous share of sermons about hell in my life. Most of them reminded me to get my spiritual ducks in a row, lest I end up in a very hot place. "Confess that Jesus is Lord tonight!" would boom the evangelist. "You might get hit by a car on your way home." Those messages always *scared the hell out of me*. I would imagine my eternity in a scalding-hot place, bartering for a sip of water to appease my thirst. So I confessed my sins and pleaded for God's mercy—more than once, I might add.

But as Professor Warheim argued, the Christian life is not simply to prepare for eternity. We need to have courage to cross the road and confront those who make life a living hell for others.

Unfortunately, too much of contemporary, popular-TV Christian theology advocates that the *blessed life* is a life without fear. God's blessing is equated with financial success, an absence of stress, and an abundance of leisure. We go to church to avoid the "evils" of the world, to escape *from* the hellish aspects of our existence. Church becomes our sanctuary—a place where we can shut out the confusion and chaos of our society. Consequently, being a Christian turns into a vocation of seeking uninterrupted security. We move our churches to the suburbs, live in gated communities, shop at exclusive stores. The last thing we want to think about is going to a place that will cause us to be afraid.

So how do we reconcile these two divergent views of what it means to be a vital, caring Christian? Is Warheim right? Is his challenge to go to hell just for those going into the profession of ministry? Or is it for everyone who professes Jesus as Lord? Is the blessed Christian life a life of favor, entitlement, and security, or is it a life that calls us to go to our Egypt in our effort to liberate those whom God loves so dearly? I think we can learn a lot from Moses.

MOSES, THE CALL, AND THE FEAR OF HELL

"O Lord, please send someone else to do it."

I don't blame Moses for his response to God's challenge.

One day Moses was in the desert, a diligent son-in-law tending his father-in-law Jethro's flock of sheep. He had a predictable daily routine: wake up, eat a little breakfast, gather the sheep, lead them toward food and water. Possibly during those hours when the sheep were contentedly grazing, he'd do a little wood carving. Boring? Maybe.

But then the tranquility and predictability of his life was interrupted. Moses was asked—by no less than God—to leave his little heaven on earth and begin a journey to what would become the depths of hell.

I love Moses' reluctant honesty. The biblical and historical, but often blemished, people God used in order to transform the world were just like us. The biblical writers could have covered up the clay feet and warts of these heroes, but instead they let the incongruities and inconsistencies of these people's lives jump off the page. That's encouraging to me. Moses did try the diplomatic approach with God. But how can a person possibly back out of a God-given responsibility (see Exodus 3:13; 4:1, 10) without really ticking God off? Moses did not want to heed God's call to go and confront Pharaoh. The bottom line: *Moses was afraid.*

Every time I read this story, Moses' credibility goes up a few notches in my book. When asked to go into hell, Moses balked. That's believable. Like most of us in a crisis or facing a challenge, Moses' primal urge to survive surfaced. He evaluated the situation and didn't like the odds. Reasoning his way through the scenario, Moses flat out asked God, "Isn't there someone else to do it?" And who can blame Moses? For most of us a suicide mission is not our idea of fun. We would rather stay within the well-defined parameters of comfortable normalcy.

What made the difference for Moses were the promises of God. Moses' life hinged on this one point: was God's Word true? Was the promise that God made to Moses—"I will be with you" (Exodus 3:12)—something he could rely on when the heat was turned up? The issue was not so much how Moses *felt*; the real issue was what Moses would do. Would he be immobilized from carrying out his mission? Or embark on this incredible journey of liberation, despite his insecurities and doubts? Yes, Moses doubted if he had the tools, the equipment, the words, the fortitude, and the courage. But none of that really mattered. What mattered was his willingness to step out with faith and trust.

ROAD MARKER

Sometimes we have to cross the road to keep from being paralyzed forever by fear.

Moses' challenge is our challenge. Whether we are suburban parents who are petrified of the city, pastors who are reluctant to challenge our congregations to step out of the safety zone of church and into the surrounding neighborhoods, or a mission committee feeling called to take a group to an orphanage in

Africa, fear is fear. We can wonder like Moses certainly did what will happen when we venture out into new territory with powerful pharaohs causing problems along the way. And also wonder if God will truly be there as he promises. Will fear become the god that controls our destiny? Or will the promise of the presence of God be our comfort and strength?

WHAT IF MOSES HAD STAYED HOME?

I believe that God does not coerce any of us to do anything—God challenges and calls people. One of God's greatest gifts to humanity is freedom—freedom to choose love over hate, freedom to serve others or serve oneself, freedom to listen to God's voice or silence it, freedom to see or turn away. We are not puppets that God controls as the great puppeteer. Like many others throughout biblical history, Moses could have walked away from his calling. He could have chosen to die a shepherd in the Horeb wilderness.

Despite his initial resistance and trepidation, Moses caught God's bigger vision for his life and his people. He confronted his fears, chose to embrace God's promise, loaded his wife and kids on donkeys, and headed back to the place from which he had run. Moses rode back to hell, where he experienced a dimension of God's character he would never have experienced anywhere else. God's ultimate force confronted the most powerful political force on earth. With the liberation of God's people from bondage and captivity, Moses found liberation from his own fears and insecurities. Moses learned a lot in hell.

Did Moses' decision create personal problems? Absolutely. Did Moses' decision bring uninvited moments of anguish and pain? Without a doubt. Did Moses' decision make his life more complex and difficult? Emphatically, yes! But because Moses pushed through his fear, God's children were saved. If Moses had not gone back to Egypt, evil might have continued to flourish unabated. And that could have changed the whole course of history.

JESUS CONFRONTS FEAR

There are some interesting parallels between Moses and Jesus—at critical moments in both men's lives they had to confront fear and its paralyzing impact on decision making. We've examined Moses' story. For Jesus, the moment came in the garden of Gethsemane (Matthew 26:36-44). There he wrestled with the question of whether he would fulfill the ultimate act of obedience—surrendering to the inhumane torture of a Roman cross and ultimate death.

"If it is possible, may this cup be taken from me," pleaded an anguished Jesus, "Yet not as I will, but as you will" (verse 39). Matthew captures some of the most gripping and human words in the Gospels, words revealing a depth of fear and anguish that confirms Jesus' full humanity. Some biblical scholars say that this was the true moment of Jesus' incarnation—where the true Son of Man and the true Son of God intersected.

Jesus didn't want to undertake the brutality of the Cross. This prayer wasn't from a divine robot with computer chips and wires. A man possessing no affinity for human life would never have sought a plan B. Yet three times Jesus prayed to God in isolation, begging for an alternative plan to suffering on a cross. Three times he retreated from his conversation with God to seek the fellowship of his disciples, who happened to be sleeping. Jesus the man, facing the critical moment of his life, interacted with both God and friends.

Thanks be to God that fear does not triumph. Fear is surrendered to the greater will of God. Jesus demonstrated that the problem with fear is not fear; fear is part of the human condition. The problem with fear is when it dominates and controls our decisions.

ROAD MARKER

Jesus crossed the road to demonstrate how fear can be overcome.

So how do we, as followers of Jesus, deal with fear? How do we find the courage to confront road-crossing situations where we are called to stretch every fiber of our faith? This interaction in Gethsemane provides a model. First, *Jesus prayed honestly*. He did not try to hide his fear, deny it, or repress it. Jesus put it all on the table, believing that God could handle his prayer.

Second, *Jesus did not stop with prayer*. Jesus confessed his anguish and fear to his closest friends. By inviting his community of friends to experience what he felt, Jesus rejected the idea that truly spiritual people have to be superhuman. It's okay to be vulnerable and show weakness. Through this struggle Jesus garnered the fortitude needed to confront the hell that was coming—the soldiers, the beatings, the rejection, the lies, the agony of the cross. Jesus left the garden prepared for what was to come.

Fear is part of Jesus' story, because fear is part of the human condition. So let's eliminate the erroneous idea that people who are "strong" or "secure" in faith never experience fear. True people of faith confront their fears, cross their roads, and grow.

CHAPTER TEN

THE ROADBLOCK OF INDIFFERENCE

Of course, indifference can be tempting—more than that, seductive. It is so much easier to look away from victims. It is so much easier to avoid such rude interruptions to our work, our dreams, our hopes. It is, after all, awkward, troublesome, to be involved in another person's pain and despair.

ELIE WIESEL[1]

I love the story about the young pastor newly assigned to his first church. Within a week he realizes that the congregation has lost its life and vision. Weekly attendance has dwindled to a faithful remnant. Vitality is nonexistent.

Consequently, like any eager pastor, he gets on the phone and begins thumbing through the directory and calling former parishioners. Their responses are disheartening. "The church is dead," he hears again and again. "There is no life!"

Since the church has been pronounced "dead" by so many former congregants, the pastor decides to hold a funeral to "bury" the church. Enthusiastically, he invites the church board members and parishioners to attend. On that day, the sanctuary is packed; everyone has come to satisfy their curiosity.

At the front of the church is a coffin and halfway into the service the pastor invites the congregants to come up and walk past it. When they look in . . . to their surprise . . . they see themselves. The young pastor has put a mirror in the bottom of the coffin.

The crowd voices their shock and indignation. "The audacity," they cry. "What nerve!" But quickly they understand the pastor's lesson: it is *their* spiritual indifference that has infected the congregation. Their apathy killed the church.

THE DANGER OF INDIFFERENCE

Holocaust survivor and author Elie Wiesel, a Romanian Jew, witnessed and experienced the Holocaust of Nazi concentration camps in World War II. He has written over forty books with his penetrating reflections of those events, including his important books *Night* and *Dawn*. One of the great themes of his life's work is how dangerous people are who *do nothing* when they are confronted with situations that demand action.

Wiesel believes "that the opposite of love is not hate, it is indifference. The opposite of art is not ugliness, it is indifference. The opposite of faith is not heresy, it is indifference. And the opposite of life is not death, it is *indifference*. Indifference is the enemy."[2] Indifference for Wiesel means living in a state of not caring.

Most of us, without thinking, believe that the opposite of love is hate; the opposite of life is death; the opposite of beauty is ugliness. But Wiesel challenges the listener to think more deeply about the root problems we find in our world.

ROAD MARKER

Sometimes we have to cross the road to break
our habits of callous indifference.

The compelling question Wiesel raises is, why is indifference the great enemy? It is easy to conclude that Wiesel talks about indifference because he watched thousands of his Jewish friends, neighbors, and family go to the gas chamber while *good* people did nothing. *Good* people indifferently watched rather than acted. And that inaction was dangerous. The indifferent person is someone who *says nothing* and *does nothing* when he or she sees or participates in something wrong or unjust. In his 1999 Millennium Lecture, "The Perils of Indifference," which he delivered at the White House, Wiesel stated that for the indifferent person, "His or her neighbors are of no consequence."[3]

WHAT MOTIVATES A RISK TAKER?

Fortunately, not everyone during the Holocaust just stood by and watched their neighbors being gassed in the concentration camps. There were people within the communities who crossed the roads of ethnicity and religion, risking their lives for the sake of their neighbors. Why? What makes the difference between those who do nothing to help and those who risk it all?

Samuel and Pearl Oliner, a couple who did extensive research on the rescuers of Jewish Holocaust victims, were curious to understand what motivated certain non-Jewish citizens to risk so much—their lives, careers, and friends—to save Jews who were strangers to them. That had happened to Samuel Oliner himself when a Christian woman gave him refuge and changed his life forever.

In their research, the Oliners found no significant difference in the empathy scores between the rescuers and the nonrescuers. The two groups were virtually indistinguishable on such measurements as shared feelings, affection, anxiety, pleasure, humor, or susceptibility to the moods of others. But there was one difference that stood out. The rescuers had a stronger tendency to be *moved by pain.* "Sadness and helplessness aroused their empathy."[4] At some point in their lives, the rescuers had developed the capacity to connect with and to be moved by another person's pain. This connection propelled them to reach across racial and legal barriers to protect Jewish people, whether they were friends or not. Their ability to *feel* pain led to action.

When one reads the Oliners' findings, it is hard not to see a connection with one of the central teachings of Jesus—the virtue of compassion.

NEIGHBORS OF NO CONSEQUENCE

Jesus said to his disciples, "Be compassionate just as your Father is compassionate" (Luke 6:36, NJB). That verse contains significant road-crossing implications.

First, Jesus tells us flat out to be compassionate—no ifs, ands, or buts. But what does he mean by the word *compassion*?

Compassion comes from the Latin *com*, which simply means "with," and *passion*, which means "to feel." Simply put, compassion means "to feel with" other people. Some scholars believe the word *suffer* is a more accurate translation of the Latin word *passion*—which would then imply that followers of Jesus are to be people who "suffer with" other people. Regardless of how we translate the word *passion*, we are to be people who seek to walk in the shoes of others.

The second part of the verse is Jesus' affirmation of something startlingly revolutionary about the character of God. According to Jesus' teaching, God is not distant from creation and humanity. In all of God's majesty, God has the capacity to feel and suffer with men, women, children, and teens. God is compassionate; God crosses the road between heaven and humanity to feel the heartbeat of creation.

COMPASSIONATE HOLINESS

Jesus' command to "be compassionate" was very significant to the historical context in which Jesus lived and served. Jesus actually put a new spin on a command found in the Levitical code. There it calls all people of God to "be holy because I, the LORD your God, am holy" (Leviticus 19:2). Since Jesus' world was governed by what was called a holiness code, "being right with God" meant living within certain moral and religious boundaries.

The Old Testament is full of examples of what it meant to "be holy." Don't eat pork; if you do, you will be guilty of breaking the holiness code. If you work on the Sabbath, even if you are just boiling water, another part of the holiness code will be broken. If a woman is experiencing her monthly menstrual cycle, she is "unclean" and certainly not holy!

ROAD MARKER

Jesus crossed the road to walk in the shoes of others.

Being "right" with God in Jesus' day was paying attention to and keeping the list of codes and rules; after all, God was very concerned with correct external behaviors. Jesus' command to "be compassionate" rather than "be holy" puts a radical new twist on how he means his followers to live—in a way that reflected the heart of God in our day-to-day experience. And delightfully so, Jesus practiced what he preached. Frequently Jesus was described as the one who chose compassion over the holiness codes of his day. And we know that ultimately he paid the price on a cross.

Moving toward Christian maturity means so much more than rigidly adhering to a set of moral and ethical codes that protects us from another person's pain. The only way we can truly live out Jesus' command to be compassionate—"to feel with"—is to cross the road and walk in the other person's shoes.

PUTTING THE COMMAND INTO PRACTICE

Catholic writer Thomas Merton expands our understanding of compassion when he writes that there is "a keen awareness of the interdependence of all these living beings, which are all part of one another."[5] If we embrace the notion that all of life is interdependent, then we must believe that everyone is our neighbor—regardless of race, social status, or geography.

As Christians we are not free to ignore certain kinds of people or isolate ourselves from the lives of people outside our social circles. The Good Samaritan, for example, was moved by the sight of a Jewish man, viciously beaten by bandits and left on the road to die. Despite the animosity that existed between Samaritans and Jews, he could still feel compassion. The Samaritan crossed a road, stopped, and offered help to a stranger—he felt the man's pain as if it were his own. And because he could empathize with the stranger's pain, the Samaritan did not remain indifferent. He acted. He soothed the stranger's wounds with an expensive ointment and bandaged him, then took the man to an inn to be cared for.

So how can Christians move beyond our all-too-frequent attitude of indifference to become people who are compelled to challenge injustice? To speak for those who have no voice or position in society? To listen to what those who are not part of the "in group" have to say? How do Christians move from being people whose highest calling in life is not self-preservation but rather concern for others? Crossing the road has the very real potential of putting us into the shoes of another human being, which leads us towards compassion. And having a full measure of compassion invariably leads us to act in ways that change our world. Compassionate people are definitely not indifferent people.

AN UNEXPECTED BONUS

I was having a rather glorious pre-Christmas Friday—it had snowed during the previous night, and my fourteen-year-old son, Calvin, and I had briskly shoveled the walks around our ministry headquarters. I was now comfortable and warm, sitting at my familiar desk sorting through a stack of bills, junk mail, and Christmas cards. I came to an unusual, crisp envelope that looked like a fancy wedding invitation. Surprisingly, there was nothing written on the envelope other than my name scrawled in capital letters. Carefully, I inserted my stiletto opener and slit the creased edge.

When I pulled out the trifolded letter printed on cream-colored bond paper, a $22,000 check fell out!

"Dear Dr. Main, please use this gift for staff and teachers' Christmas bonuses."

I read it again and then once more, just to be sure of the donor's intent. Sure enough, unmistakably, the letter said *Christmas bonuses.*

Normally I would take a $22,000 gift and put it into the ministry's general operations account. Such a generous check would go a long way toward paying ever-present monthly bills: electricity, gas, and insurance—all the unglamorous stuff that people seldom associate with running an urban ministry. Managing cash flow in a small nonprofit is always a delicate dance. Adding to that was the fact that the two leanest months for charitable donations—January and February—were just around the corner. I was more than tempted to squirrel this little cashew away for the next time the aging building's roof leaked or the plumbing collapsed.

However, my hands were tied. This was a *designated* gift. Complying with the note's instructions was critical to my personal integrity. I knew my staff would be thrilled with a gift. I would have to grind through the winter's tough months and tap into renewed creativity that would produce more donations to take care of the everyday needs.

Equality is a significant value at our ministry. Although different staff members carry different levels of responsibility, everyone does their job without market-value compensation. With the check I held in my hand, all forty-five members of our dedicated staff would get nearly five hundred unexpected dollars in their pockets. Even after taxes, that would still be the best bonus our workers had ever received. Better than a lottery win. Plus, it would be a beautiful surprise. I could hardly wait to share the news.

Even more fun was returning from Christmas break and hearing what people did with their bonuses. "I was finally able to catch up on some bills!" said one of our teachers. "I was praying for a miracle this Christmas. My mother needed a new bed. I was able to get that for her." Someone else said, "What a great surprise—I love surprises! Thank you, thank you." The Christmas bonuses encouraged our team, and I was soon to discover much more.

DID YOU HEAR ABOUT BRENT?

"Did you hear what Brent did with *his* bonus?" whispered one of my colleagues a few days into the new year. Brent was one of our frontline youth workers, who spent his hours each week investing in and loving the kids whom most people would overlook. My colleague furtively glanced around to make sure no one was eavesdropping. Whatever she was about to divulge was not common knowledge to the rest of our community. Knowing how humble Brent was, I guessed he probably wanted to keep whatever was going on a secret.

"One of Brent's kids got locked up before Christmas," she began almost breathlessly. "It was Raheem. He got into some big trouble. He was picked up on a neighborhood drug sweep, and it was tearing Brent up to see him in jail. Brent couldn't bear eating Christmas turkey and having an eggnog while Raheem was in jail."

Sadly this scenario happens too frequently in our city; it's almost a daily occurrence with our young men. Their adolescent years can be eclipsed in the blink of an eye. Their still-developing lives are broken by merely standing in the wrong place at the wrong time. Certainly they're not all innocent bystanders. But such episodes set in motion a staggering spiral of events that can push someone from a path of success onto a path of destruction and apathy.

Our workers love, serve, mentor, and pray for these kids year after year. Too frequently our dedicated staff have their hearts broken because of a random cruel situation.

Now with songs of the season's peace on earth and goodwill toward humanity becoming fainter, Brent's favorite kid—Raheem—was sitting in jail without even a glimmer of hope of being released. Brent knew that without the services of someone who could make the appropriate legal maneuvers, his young friend would be tagged with a record that would scar his life ambitions and that he would have to survive in a crowded, smelly cell with tough, hard-core kids.

Brent called several local law firms to get a price for services; the answer was always the same—five hundred dollars.

"Guess what?" whispered my inside source. I knew what was coming next but gave her the pleasure of finishing the story. "Brent took his Christmas bonus, paid for a lawyer, and Raheem got out on bail for the holidays!"

For a young man like Brent, living on a meager missionary salary, to give away 100 percent of his Christmas bonus was purely an act of bare-knuckle sacrifice. Most of us would prefer to stay on our safe side of the road, avoiding a relationship with a high-risk person who might cause us to dip into our resources. Like the Good Samaritan, Brent crossed the road even though it cost him time, resources, and emotional energy. He followed his heart. Road crossing challenges us to act in ways that defy convention.

TURNING YOUR BACK

It's obvious that the dangerous thing about crossing roads is that it is costly. To allow ourselves to "feel with" another person and to move beyond our chronic indifference taxes our time, our finances, and certainly our energies. But isn't that precisely the cost of following Jesus? Isn't that precisely the dimension of discipleship that says, "Take up your cross and follow me"?

As I am writing this, newspapers abound with stories about the vast sums of money made on Wall Street. Year-end bonuses for money managers have spiraled into the stratosphere; top-of-the-line luxury models at Porsche, Lamborghini, and BMW dealerships are all back-ordered. Exclusive vacation resorts, of course, are having a banner season. Cartier, Coach, and Neiman Marcus report that they have finished their fiscal years on high notes. Santa Claus, bless his ho ho ho, arrived this year on Wall Street with his sleigh chockablock full of goodies for all the good boy and girl investors who successfully made the wealthy wealthier.

ROAD MARKER

Sometimes we have to cross the road and
give our Christmas bonuses away.

I wonder what kind of impact those extravagant bonuses had on the struggling charities of our country. Perhaps there were some year-end tax write-offs, but my guess is that those who did not choose to share from their abundance were too busy or too indifferent to cross a road, to allow their hearts to be broken by the needs of others.

Brent would not have been able to enjoy his anonymous Christmas gift when it dawned on him that his surprise bonus could buy freedom for someone he had dared to care about. Gifts we give to God have a curious way of coming back to us in ways that stagger our imagination and delight our souls. I think in God's eyes, Raheem's smile as he practically skipped out of jail on Christmas Eve was right up there with the joyous shepherds' smiles as they gazed on the newborn Christ child. For all of them, a magnificent gift had been given that produced more joy than anything Wall Street could ever offer.

That Christmas Eve night, Brent moved closer to the heart of Jesus. And Raheem—well, I can assure you, he has never forgotten his gift of unexpected grace.

CHAPTER ELEVEN

THE ROADBLOCK OF MISGUIDED THEOLOGY

Away with the noise of your songs!

AMOS 5:23

I frequently hear comments about people being blessed. "God has really blessed me," exclaims my friend over a cup of coffee. "Look, I've got a healthy family, a great job, two family vacations a year, and only one more kid to get through college. How much better can it get?"

"Profits at the firm are really up this year," says Jane, smiling. "Looks like we're all going to get some pretty big year-end bonuses. God *is* good! What a blessing!"

"I'm the only one in the company to survive the latest round of layoffs. God has blessed me in a big way."

Most of us hear statements like these all the time—during coffee hour at church, in Bible study, while chitchatting on the phone. Our friends give God the credit for their success and fortune; sure, they acknowledge their hard work, but they are not arrogant enough to believe that hard work equates to financial success. After all, there are many people who work hard and never seem to catch a break.

But from these conversations and others like them, I am coming to this conclusion: most people equate God's blessing and God's favor with financial stability, health, opportunities for leisure, and a lack of difficulty in their lives. They point to passages from the Old Testament as proof that prosperity is a sure sign of God's favor. "He who trusts in the LORD will prosper," comes the exhortation from Proverbs 28:25. And from the psalmist: "Blessed are all who fear the LORD . . . blessings and prosperity will be yours" (Psalm 128:1-2). One can make a pretty strong case that prosperity is a blessing from God.

But what about statements like these:

"Where is God? I just never seem to get a break." "I tithe faithfully and God doesn't seem to do anything. Every month is a struggle to make ends meet." "Why did God allow me to lose my job? I work hard. Attend church. Volunteer my time." I'm sure you've heard these comments, maybe even more often than the former ones. Or maybe you've said them yourself to God or posed them to your friends during times of difficulty and stress.

Let's be honest: when life gets tough, many of us begin to question God's presence and involvement in our lives. What have I done wrong? Why is God punishing me? When will God notice me? If we buy into a theology that God is the author of our "blessings," then it's likely we will also buy into a theology that blames God when he doesn't come through for us.

Recently a mother walked into my office in tears. She couldn't pay her electric bill, and the power was about to be cut off. She wasn't a slacker. She worked two jobs, was doing her best to raise two boys, and was a faithful member of a local church. "Why is God doing this to me?" she cried, her head on my desk. "I go to church. I'm trying to do right by my boys, and I tithe 10 percent of my income." What was I supposed to say? I was at a loss for words. All I could offer was a little money from our benevolence fund.

Whenever I am tempted to support a point by an Old Testament scriptural proof-text, it just does not work in the larger biblical story. Relying on this kind of formulaic approach sets us up for all kinds of problems when trying to define our relationship with God. How we *feel* about God becomes conditional on our life circumstances.

But there is a deeper problem—a problem that has severe consequences for our world and God's witness in the world.

Equating God's blessing with financial stability, minimal problems, abundant leisure, and a successful career means that we will intentionally avoid that part of the Christian experience that calls us to go to those hellish places on earth to confront evil. Why would we pursue anything that might compromise that "blessed" existence? We will consciously, or even unconsciously, travel a path of least resistance.

Our theology of blessing deeply impacts the way we live out our faith each day.

SORRY TO RAIN ON THE PARADE

I'll be the first to admit that I like to get a paycheck every two weeks. Having a little extra cash at the end of the month to take my wife out to dinner certainly enhances our marriage. Having a car I can rely on to start most mornings makes the commute to work a little less stressful. Having neighbors who don't make a lot of noise makes it easier to get a good night's sleep. And I am certainly not going to complain about an older furnace that fires up on a cold New Jersey winter day. But if this is my idea of the blessed life I have misread the Scriptures.

ROAD MARKER

Jesus crossed the road and threw out the preconceived
notions of what a blessed life looked like.

Don't get me wrong. It's important to thank God for these provisions and many more. But if my whole life revolves around preserving these comforts at the expense of other human beings, then I think I am misguided in my interpretation of what it means to follow Jesus.

The last time I checked Jesus' travel itinerary, he avoided the glitzy seaside resorts and instead went to places where people were in difficult situations. Unlike other religious leaders who sought a place to be sequestered from the influences of the world, Jesus gravitated toward crowds and public places. Jesus established his ministry in Capernaum, a backwater town known for its poverty. He traveled the highways and byways, embracing lepers and the sick, demonstrating that his message about the love of God was more than talking points shared within the four walls of the local synagogue. He confronted religious authorities who wielded their power in ways that made life hell for those who were subject to their leadership. To top it all off, he walked into the heart of the city that opposed him most vehemently: Jerusalem. Rather than preserving his life, Jesus chose to lose it.

So did Jesus lead a blessed life?

Using our contemporary Western understanding of blessing, I'd have to say no. Jesus owned no property; he put mission above comfort, which often meant certain duress. And he ended up hanging from a cross on a garbage heap between two thieves. You call that a blessing?

Essentially, to Jesus' listening audience, it must have seemed that he was throwing the Old Testament notions of the blessed life to the wind.

A NEW IDEA OF BLESSED

Nowhere does Jesus assault our contemporary understanding of blessing more than in the Beatitudes found in Luke 6. Here the idea of a "blessed" life is turned on its head.

Blessed are you who are poor,
for yours is the kingdom of God.

Blessed are you who are hungry now,
   for you will be filled.
Blessed are you who weep now,
   for you will laugh.
   Blessed are you when people hate you, and when they
exclude you, revile you, and defame you on account of
the Son of Man. (Luke 6:20-22, NRSV, emphasis added)

If you were poor, hungry, sad, hated, and rejected, would you
consider yourself blessed? Most of us would emphatically say no!
If you were economically poor, wouldn't you want to reevaluate
your job situation? If you were sad, you might consider sched-
uling an appointment with a therapist. If a friend said hateful
things about you, wouldn't you want to delete him or her from
your phone "faves"? And yet Jesus argues that people in these
circumstances are the blessed ones.

I can imagine the heads spinning among the people who were
there, hearing Jesus in person. But Jesus doesn't stop there. He
pushes it even more:

But woe to you who are rich,
   for you have already received your comfort.
Woe to you who are well fed now,
   for you will go hungry.
Woe to you who laugh now,
   for you will mourn and weep.
   Woe to you when all men speak well of you, for that is
how their fathers treated the false prophets. (Luke 6:24-26,
emphasis added)

Come on, Jesus! You've got to be kidding. Everything I have been
taught to value is up for grabs in these statements. If this is your

idea of blessing, Jesus, why would anyone want to be part of your program? But Jesus was just warming up to his bigger message.

Luke's Gospel provides further details of what it means to join the Jesus program. The kind of faith Jesus calls his followers to make a part of their lives is a faith that has *nothing* to do with escapism, avoidance, and spiritual experiences that make us feel good. It is a faith that defies human sensibilities and human self-interest. I have taken the liberty to paraphrase and add the italicized lines to the following Scriptures, simply to emphasize what Jesus expects from those who believe in him.

> *Cross the road toward* your enemies and do good to those who hate you. (Luke 6:27)
> *Cross the road toward* those who will not necessarily love you back. (Luke 6:32)
> *Cross the road toward* the demons and diseased people, and preach the Good News (without money, bag, bread, or extra clothing). (Luke 9:3)
> *Cross the road toward* Jerusalem, the place that will resist and kill you. (Luke 9:51)
> *Cross the road toward* Samaria, the place where you will not be welcomed. (Luke 9:52-53)
> *Cross the road toward* the "wolves," and tell them that the Kingdom of God is near. (Luke 10:3)

The Jesus program is about running toward the things most of us would like to avoid—things that take time, energy, pain, courage, faith, and vision. But according to Jesus, we might enter into the realm of blessing if we move in this direction.

SONGS JESUS WOULD NEVER SING

It isn't only culturally biased biblical interpretation that may convince us to avoid things Jesus wants us to embrace. Even our expressions of worship can be a barrier that steers us away from the path Jesus calls us to walk. Both the Old Testament prophets and Jesus have a few words to say about the nature and purpose of true worship.

Take Amos, for example. I doubt if he was ever asked to be a guest preacher, because he had the uncanny ability to define *authentic* faith. From his writings, you can tell that the little sheep-herder from Tekoa packed a punch when he spoke. In a few chapters he made it perfectly clear that God is never impressed with our worship if our actions are disconnected from promoting good.

"Away with the noise of your songs!" he cried (Amos 5:23) to those who showed up in their Sabbath best to sing thirty minutes of praise and worship. These sincere worshipers had just closed their ears to those who spoke truth (verse 10), trampled the poor (verse 11), taken bribes (verse 12), and made sure the poor were denied justice in the courtroom (verse 12). "Shut up!" cries Amos. Worship that is disconnected from alleviating people's hell on earth is not authentic worship. True worship, according to the prophets, is about making sure vulnerable people are cared for and that the actions of the ones who govern reflect the heart and nature of God.

A good friend of mine named Ed heads up a ministry that fixes houses for the poor and elderly. People who have neither the financial means nor the physical ability to get the job done call Ed. He has seen some pretty deplorable living conditions in his years as a hammer-slinging missionary. A leaking roof? Rotting stairs? Faulty wiring? No problem; Ed will take care of it. From the Mississippi Delta to the backwoods of Arkansas, Ed has seen it all.

One day Ed and I were sitting on top of a roof banging shingles together. It was a particularly hot day, and I was not having much fun. But Ed leaned over and said, "This is worship to me. I feel closest to God when I have a hammer in hand, my tool belt around my waist, and sweat on my brow, helping folk." Amos would have liked Ed.

ROAD MARKER

Sometimes we have to cross the road and worship God
with a hammer in hand and sweat on our brow.

Jesus had a few things to say about true worship also. When
the religious leaders tried to rebuke Jesus and his disciples for
not "keeping" the Sabbath—not worshiping in correct ways—
Jesus reminded them that God desires "mercy, not sacrifice"
(Matthew 12:7) and that "it is lawful to do good on the Sabbath"
(12:12). For Jesus, Sabbath worship was not about following the
correct rules, showing displays of piety, putting the big offering
in the plate, or singing the right songs. For Jesus, authentic worship was acting in ways that were consistent with the abundant
life-giving ways of God. So when a man with a withered hand
and a diminished sense of self-worth showed up on the Sabbath
for healing, Jesus engaged in an act of worship—he healed him!

The God of life made the Sabbath and worship for the good
of humanity, not the other way around. Upholding a pharisaical
notion of worship and Sabbath-keeping while those around you
suffer isn't part of Jesus' vision statement of what it means to
commune with God. Jesus' vision aligns itself more with the
prophet Isaiah who writes: "Is not this the kind of fasting I have
chosen: to loose the chains of injustice and untie the cords of the
yoke, to set the oppressed free . . . to share your food with the
hungry and to provide the poor wanderer with shelter. . . . Then
your righteousness will go before you" (Isaiah 58:6-8).

Sometimes when I am singing hymns and worship songs
in church, I wonder if Jesus would sing the song I am singing.
We all have our old favorites that bring up all kinds of warm
memories. This is not a bad thing. But if you really look at the
lyrics to some of our songs, you could wonder if Jesus would
nudge you between stanzas—"Nice tune, but can you believe

these words—this has *nothing* to do with my mission" or "They missed the point entirely on that one!" or "Why do they only sing about what I did on the cross—what about the rest of my life, my ministry?"

Do we really think that Jesus, who spent his time reminding religious authorities about authentic faith, would sing our worship songs that only direct our attention heavenward, rather than compel us to embrace our neighbor and integrate our faith in solving the problems of the world? Would Jesus only sing songs that celebrate his divinity and lordship ("Fairest Lord Jesus, ruler of all nations"), and yet never mention his humanity, his humility, or his compassion?

Would he sing only songs that constantly talked about loving God in some abstract pseudo-psychological fashion ("Draw me close to you, never let me go"), yet never talk about loving God through the way we treat the least of these? I think Jesus would have a hard time with some of our worship songs. I think he might question worship that makes clear demarcations between the sacred and the secular, leading worshipers away from dealing with the here and now.

I raise the question about worship and our understanding of the Sabbath because it is made evident throughout Scripture that the length of our fasts, the sweetness of our singing during our praise-and-worship time, and the size of our tithes do not impress God. Worship, without actions consistent with the teachings of Jesus, doesn't cut it in the Jesus program.

A DIVINE DISCONNECTION

What Jesus so wonderfully models is a unity of the spiritual and the day-to-day. There was no "spiritual life" squeezed in for Jesus—his whole life was a spiritual enterprise. In contemporary America it is easy to compartmentalize our lives. Family life, job life, volunteer life, church life, and personal spiritual life can easily be lived with little integration and connection among each other.

And yet the overarching message of Jesus suggests that we cannot live as compartmentalized people. Our spiritual lives must integrate real engagement in a real world that isn't always nice.

We all know, however, that good theology does not necessarily guarantee actions consistent with beliefs we claim to hold close. We can have an airtight theology yet fail to implement those truths in our lives. But there are powerful examples of people who have chosen to make road crossing part of their spiritual disciplines. It has transformed their lives, their churches, and their worlds.

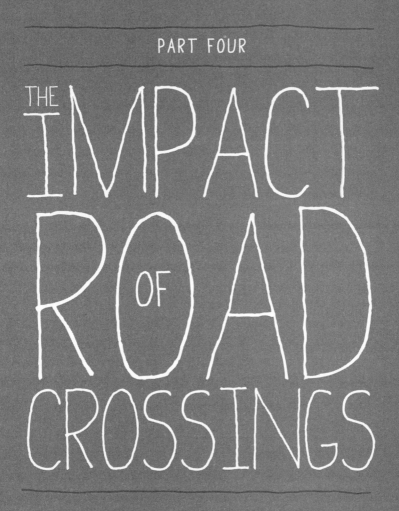

PART FOUR

THE IMPACT OF ROAD CROSSINGS

CHAPTER TWELVE

SECOND-FLOOR CHRISTIANITY AND THE ART OF EMBRACE

*In my case . . . encounters have been responsible
for new departures in my life.*

PAUL TOURNIER[1]

"You've got to get to the second floor to really understand what's going on," began Tom.

"What?" I asked as I looked incredulously at my friend. He was bundled in a down quilt, his withered face peering out like an Eskimo in a parka. Tom was in the last days of his waning life. He had spent a year battling brain cancer, heroically fighting through chemotherapy, alternative medicines, and a strict diet, but new cancer spots kept appearing on his CAT scans. I sensed that this was going to be our last conversation.

"Most people never get to the second floor," Tom continued. He was barely lucid, but at that moment his eyes focused on me with an intense and piercing concentration. He whispered, "That's where you can see how people really live. That's where you see the poverty." Was he speaking metaphorically or literally? I wasn't sure—perhaps a little of both.

Tom had spent three years with our ministry back in the late 1990s. He'd been sort of an odd fit, actually. A carpenter by trade, he spent most of his life on a commune before stumbling into a church one Sunday and hearing a pastor preach on grace. The message changed his life, resulting in a desire to put his faith into some kind of service; he just wasn't sure what. But it quickly became apparent that Tom had an uncanny ability to *connect* with people, to see their real story. Pastors could not come close to Tom's unconventional relational abilities; he could have easily taught a seminary course on pastoral care.

"The living room usually presents the best side of us." It was taking more time for him to get the words out now. "It's the public face, sorta like old Ms. Sheldon's neat and tidy but modest front room. The living room's usually respectable. But on the second floor, now that was a different story. Sixteen people, mostly kids, slept there; the ceiling leaked, the bathroom was rotted, the kids slept on the floor on urine-stained mattresses. It was awful! That's where I really saw the poverty." His gray eyes were glazed from an unpleasant memory.

Ms. Sheldon, I knew, was an impoverished grandmother who lived up the street. I was aware that she struggled, but I had no idea of the hidden severity of what she daily confronted. A number of Gramma Sheldon's own children had gone down the wrong path, leaving her with their unwanted children to care for. Her grandchildren, nephews, and nieces all ended up at her house— on the second floor. Tom had befriended Gramma Sheldon and was mentoring one of her grandchildren.

"One day I was invited to see the second floor," he said with an eternal weariness. "That was my right of passage. It had taken me close to a year to build trust by just hanging out. But I was allowed out of the living room and up the flight of stairs to see the other reality. Gramma Sheldon's effort to navigate the worn, steep steps was heroic . . . and painful."

He paused a moment to catch his breath, then requested a sip of water from a plastic cup sitting beside the rumpled bed. Tom sucked on the straw as I held the cup to his parched mouth. It was hard to believe that Tom was once a man who could carry stacks of shingles up thirty-foot ladders without breaking a sweat.

He could hang a fifty-pound piece of double-thick Sheetrock single-handedly. Now he could barely summon the strength to sip water through a bent straw.

"I decided to call it *second-floor* Christianity," he whispered. (Did I detect a glint in his eye?) "You see, Bruce, most of us never get beyond the first floor. We seldom are trusted enough to see what's upstairs; seldom are patient enough to see what's beneath the surface, what the real world's like."

Second-floor Christianity. I'd never heard anyone put it that way before. But I knew exactly what he meant. Sure, I've crossed roads and gone into all sorts of houses, but seldom have I been invited to the secret, off-limits second floor . . . the floor where people really live. I have assessed situations based on a quick glance, but did I have the whole picture? Now looking back, I think that too often I failed horribly to understand the deeper issues and the problems. It can be easy to cross roads; it's much more difficult to connect in a way that allows us to get to the second floor.

ROAD MARKER

Sometimes we have to cross the road and wait
for an invitation to see what's off-limits.

When Tom finally saw Ms. Sheldon's second floor, he had her complete trust. Tom did not sweep in as some savior; he knew that he had to spend enough time in the living room before Ms. Sheldon felt secure. Tom listened and cared. And slowly, as that trust grew, the two of them developed a plan to overhaul the second floor.

Tom mobilized a group of volunteers to come and fix the sad, disheveled second floor. Ms. Sheldon shared her good cookin' and hospitality as Tom's group of carpenters, interior designers, and tradesmen worked to create a place where children and great-grandchildren could sleep in rooms that did not leak. Carpets were laid, bunk beds were built, new mattresses purchased.

None of this good work would have ever happened if Tom had been impatient. Gramma Sheldon needed to hear about Tom's "second floor"—his failed marriage, his destructive involvement with a cult, his earlier problems with drugs—before ascending the steps with Tom in her own house.

Many of us never get to the second floor. We miss the richer story. There is no formula that guarantees our efforts to cross the road will yield all kinds of wonderful insights and growth. But there is a model I've discovered that can provide a framework—a language—to help guide us through the process.

A GUIDE TO AUTHENTIC ROAD CROSSING

Miroslav Volf, a Croatian-born theologian, knows what it means to cross roads with integrity. Volf watched ethnic conflicts rip apart the fabric of the former Yugoslavia, and he grappled with the Christian teachings of loving one's neighbor where horrendous, hate-filled acts were being committed between brothers and sisters because of race, religion, and ethnicity. When Serbian fighters raped women, killed innocent civilians, and burned churches, Volf was often confronted with the question: could he love a *cetnik*—one of these fighters? That question captures the ultimate tension of road-crossing Christianity.

Volf is not a disconnected academic. He comments, "If you just analyze religion, you're doing good work, but socially you're inconsequential. You're not shaping the world."[2] In his book *Exclusion and Embrace: A Theological Exploration of Identity, Otherness, and Reconciliation*, Volf provides a model important for those interested in reaching across borders and connecting in a way that truly brings about transformation.

Picture two people hugging one another, Volf says, quickly pointing out that he is not interested in the physical embrace itself.[3] It's his metaphor for what it means to connect with another human being in a way that leads to deeper understanding, mutual respect, potential reconciliation, an expanded spiritual vision, and an enlarged sense of self. I believe it's a model of engagement that can help us become Christians who get to the "second floor."

Volf describes four natural stages when two people encounter one another, and each one is critical if understanding is to occur between two different parties.

The first stage is to simply *open our arms*. This doesn't necessarily mean to stand with our arms spread out like a bird in full flight. Rather, it means opening and preparing our hearts and minds to receive the other person.

The second stage is to *wait*. This is hard for most of us who want to rush in and help. Shouldn't we just slather the love of Jesus on another human, whether the person is ready for us or not? No, says Volf. Be patient. The embrace needs to be mutual and reciprocated.

Third, *give the other person a hug*. Not a smothering or crushing bearlike kind of hug that overpowers the other person. You need to feel their hug too.

Finally, says Volf, *let go*, and allow the person to retain his or her individuality and uniqueness.[4] This model of embrace can be extremely helpful as we prepare ourselves to cross roads.

JESUS AND THE ACT OF EMBRACE

In chapter four we looked at Jesus' encounter with Bartimaeus. Not only is it an excellent example of Jesus crossing the road to the poor, I think it also exemplifies Volf's fourfold embrace model.

Stage One: Opening Your Arms

"Jesus stopped and said, 'Call him'" (Mark 10:49).

Sitting by a dusty road, day after day, year after year, relying on the charity of those who walked busily past must have been dehumanizing for Bartimaeus. I'm sure he heard a lot of interesting conversations—lovers' quarrels, business deals, parental reprimands, and the village gossip. But I doubt he was ever invited into any of these conversations. Presumably the only acknowledgment he ever received was the occasional tinkling of a coin—enough to buy a few morsels of bread at the end of the day. Mother Teresa would have said that Bartimaeus epitomized the poverty of being nobody to anybody.

But one day, a man *stopped*.

Stopped . . . dead in his tracks.

Jesus.

Earlier in the chapter, Jesus had pronounced his own death. His days were numbered, and time was of the essence. With the clock ticking, wouldn't you think Jesus needed to impart those final pearls of wisdom to his A team, complete those sermon outlines, write his books, and have power talks with those who could carry on his legacy? Instead, Jesus stopped for a blind beggar— someone who held little social significance. Jesus opened his arms to a person with an anonymous voice on the side of the road and extended an invitation for an embrace.

Surely Jesus could have just donated a few coins out of the treasury box or waved his finger in a healing gesture. But Jesus refused a hurried act of charity. He said emphatically, "Call him." By stopping and calling Bartimaeus, Jesus opened his arms.

Stage Two: Waiting

"What do you want me to do for you?" (Mark 10:51).

This is fascinating to me. Rather than imposing his agenda on the man by offering Bartimaeus money, food, or healing, Jesus made no assumptions as to what the man's needs were. He wanted to hear it straight from Bartimaeus. So Jesus asked the question and then waited.

This stage of *waiting* demonstrates how well-intentioned Christians should approach those who have been marginalized and pushed to the outskirts of society. By asking Bartimaeus, "What do you want me to do for you?" Jesus believed the blind beggar wanted more than to receive people's charity for the rest of his life. Bartimaeus didn't ask for a pot of gold, a new house, or even to be moved to the prime begging location. He wanted a different kind of life as a full participant in his community.

Christians often miss this critical step. I remember talking to a youth pastor of an affluent church who decided that people in our city needed winter coats. So with a station wagon full of donated coats, he drove into a neighborhood and began knocking on doors. "I have new coats for you!" he shared enthusiastically. To his surprise, doors were slammed in his face after curt words were said. The youth pastor returned home with a station wagon full of coats.

He had made an assumption: everyone in the poor community absolutely needed a winter coat, and none of the residents had any pride, might like a particular style, or might want to work for their own coat. His impatient compassion and top-down approach diminished the worth of the persons whom he wanted to help. Trust and friendship never developed. Rather than asking the question, "What can I do for you?" this youth pastor just assumed everyone needed what he wanted to give. Waiting involves patience and listening. When Jesus asked Bartimaeus a question, he was willing to wait for an answer.

ROAD MARKER

Jesus crossed the road to honor a beggar,
acknowledging his infinite value.

Second-floor Christianity can happen only when our immediate urges to help are reined in and waiting is exercised. Over the years I have seen many Christians with open arms come to the inner city or travel to developing countries to do good things in the name of Jesus. Their arms may be open, but their zeal to make a difference negates the voice and presence of those they are trying to help. It often becomes the rich doing charity for those poor people. Nobody grows through the embrace. Nobody has his or her perspectives changed.

My friend Tom spent many afternoons sipping iced tea in Gramma Sheldon's living room, asking questions and developing a friendship. When she was ready, she allowed Tom to enter the space that had been shielded from the outside world. Like Bartimaeus talking with Jesus, she eventually revealed her deeper need.

Stage Three: Embracing One Another
"Your faith has healed you" (Mark 10:52).

Within the Christian tradition there has been a tendency to "fix" people and shape them into the image of those who have come to "help." The history of missions is wrought with examples of missionaries shaping and making people into their own image of Christians. Ancient cultures, traditions, dress, music, art, and stories have been tragically erased because of zealous people— most often pious Europeans and Westerners—who believed their vision of the Christian life embodied absolute truth. Volf clearly advocates that authentic road crossers do not want to diminish the identities of the people they embrace, nor do they want to completely surrender their own unique personalities and identities. "One needs to maintain the boundaries of the self, but also keep the boundaries porous," instructs Volf. "Fundamentalism is a hardening of the boundaries. I want to keep them porous."[5]

The Scriptures don't tell us whether Jesus and Bartimaeus actually physically hugged each other when their conversation concluded. However, it is apparent that Jesus had no desire to exercise charity in a way that diminished Bartimaeus as a human being who was uniquely made in the image of God. Jesus said to

Bartimaeus, "Your faith has healed you." Can you imagine hearing these words if you were a poor, dependent human being who had never been given the opportunity to contribute or share?

Jesus upheld Bartimaeus as an example of faith; he uncovered, affirmed, and revealed to everyone in the crowd the one gift this blind man did possess—the gift of faith. Bartimaeus may seem like he had nothing: no mutual funds, no 401(k), no seat on a city council, no ballparks named in his honor. But Bartimaeus had faith, and the story of that faith is remembered for perpetuity. I believe even Jesus went on his way with a gift— a glimpse of authentic faith.

Stage Four: Letting Go

"'Go,' said Jesus" (Mark 10:52).

"Go"—one simple, but loaded, instruction. Although he certainly could have, Jesus didn't recruit Bartimaeus as a poster child for his growing ministry. Jesus was not a cult leader demanding that Bartimaeus relinquish his individuality and freedom. Jesus was not an egocentric, charismatic head honcho who needed the continual affirmation and praise of his subjects. Jesus said, "Move on. Live your life and share your story. Go!"

I appreciate Volf's emphasis on letting go of those whom we have crossed the road to embrace. Neither Jesus nor Volf suggests that we are supposed to pitch a tent and forever live on the other side of the road. Our "hugs" have time limits. Our encounters are not forever. Rather than assimilating our identities with the other people, our identities are expanded as we leave their presence with a new perspective. Talk about exciting!

This idea captures the vision God has for humanity. Cultural, racial, economic, and geographic differences make us distinct from one another. God's vision for humanity is not to assimilate into one homogeneous tribe. Our distinctiveness is celebrated and affirmed as our borders are more porous and receptive.

Bartimaeus watched Jesus leave and knew he was a different man because of a few moments of Jesus' time. Healed? Absolutely. But also a man who had been heard and empowered to share his life-changing experience with others.

CALLING ALL SECOND-FLOOR CHRISTIANS

"I came to fix these kids," confessed Rick, the middle-aged man standing in the corner of the youth center. It was volunteer appreciation night at our urban ministry. I had opened the floor to our special guests to share their recent experiences.

But Rick wasn't the first to speak. Minutes before, an eleventh grader named Cassandra had shared how her tutor had impacted her life. Cassandra had learned the rudiments of chemistry from Rick.

All eyes were on Rick as he continued. "But now I realize that I've been fixed." His eyes welled with tears.

"It's been a tough year for me," he explained. "My two adolescent sons are giving me trouble. My younger brother passed away tragically." The room was dead silent.

"I've learned about courage, pain, and perseverance from these young people. I can honestly say that I would not have made it without these kids. They've helped me realize that I needed fixing. Thank you." Weekly tutoring sessions with a teenager raised in challenging circumstances had changed Rick. He had come to teach, but Cassandra had become the teacher. During their times together, they had solved chemistry problems but had also talked about life and personal struggles. It wasn't long before Rick had realized that Cassandra had things to offer him. Courage. Perseverance. Simple gratitude.

ROAD MARKER

Sometimes we have to cross the road and keep
our mouths shut and our arms open.

Rick definitely opened his arms initially to Cassandra; Rick crossed the road. But he came in with an "I can fix what's broken here" attitude. The waiting, listening, and learning parts were the hard parts for him. Would he be patient enough to let the young woman he tutored speak into his life?

Our brokenness often helps us cross roads with a greater depth of compassion. That was the case with Rick. Rather than coming in once a week to fix the kids in the program, negating their contributions and voices, Rick eventually came to a place where he received the mutual embraces of the youth he came to change. This made all the difference.

Miroslav Volf's model of embracing provides an important structure for people wanting to increase the probability of truly life-changing road-crossing experiences. He provides no magic formula guaranteeing that every road-crossing encounter is going to catapult participants to new spiritual heights. Volf's four acts of embrace simply offer a language and theology that *can* lead God's people to the "second floor"—those places where true reconciliation and a broader vision for justice, compassion, and understanding can be discovered. Even with no guarantee, it is critical that we try. As second-floor Christians our eyes and hearts will be opened to insights, perspectives, and realities that most people fail to see. As second-floor Christians who have built trust out of our authenticity and patience, we can begin to peel back the protective veneer that so much of the world hides behind and begin to address real issues in a way that affirms the dignity of all people.

CHAPTER THIRTEEN

ROAD-CROSSING ADVENTURES: A BUSINESSMAN, A PASTOR, A LAWYER, AND A VETERINARIAN

But all of us must also have one foot in our faith
community and one foot in the larger world—
or frankly we have little to offer either group.
. . . Somehow we all must learn to love people,
groups, and institutions that really turn
us off—or love is not love at all.

RICHARD ROHR

"Let's cross over to the other side of the lake," Jesus said to his disciples.

Imagine the responses of his inner circle of followers. "Aw, come on, Jesus," Peter complains. "The boys are tired. We've all been on our feet since before sunrise."

James, the beginnings of his doubt emerging, joins in. "This really isn't a great time to travel. But you know that. Those squalls rise in the blink of an eye, and we have no dry clothes with us."

Jesus says nothing. Still muttering, the weary men reluctantly climb into their boat and head out.

It had been another long day for Jesus and his disciples—Jesus teaching, explaining, and talking with the crowds; the disciples explaining, talking, and doing crowd control. Jesus' parables and illustrations revealed both creative and often perplexing insights to the crowds and even to his disciples. So at the end of the day, everyone in the Jesus camp wanted some rest around a campfire and a little freshly caught fried fish, a happy debriefing of the day's events, and most of all, a good night's rest on the banks of the Galilee.

But Jesus was insistent. "Let us go over to the other side" (Mark 4:35). What was on the other side that was so important? A resort with hot tubs? Sympathetic crowds? Maybe a little solitude?

No.

On the other side was Decapolis.

Decapolis (meaning Ten Cities) was a center for decadent paganism, not orthodox religious purity. Decapolis was located in that part of Israel that had been most influenced by early Greek and Roman thought. It was the eastern frontier of the Roman Empire, where most pious spiritual leaders would have been mortified to be seen. Everything about it seemed opposed to the new vision of peace, justice, and compassion that Jesus was sharing. The young men on the boat knew that setting sail to the other side meant more work. This was not going to be any vacation.

Their suspicions proved accurate: after arriving in Decapolis Jesus faced one confrontation after another—a demon-possessed man, an inquiring religious leader, and a defiled peasant woman. But each confrontation was also a transforming encounter. Jesus reminded his disciples that following God was never a license to live in isolation or detachment; the faith of these young and eager men was being stretched, and their understanding of what it meant to participate in God's new, iconoclastic movement in the world was becoming clearer.

Jesus' charge—let's go to the other side—still reverberates across the centuries and offers a jarring reminder that a faith journey usually involves dynamic confrontations that cause vibrant growth. As we push off every day into the world, like

Jesus' disciples, we open ourselves to new growth opportunities and to God's Spirit working in and through us. Lake crossings and road crossings are the core part of discipleship curriculum.

Are you ready to cross a lake or a road with Jesus? It's definitely an adventure. One that the following four people experienced firsthand. Here are their stories.

A BUSINESSMAN: LOVING YOUR COMPETITION

If you love those who love you,
what credit is that to you?

LUKE 6:32

"I had an incredible meeting this morning," said my friend Rob.

Rob, a college buddy, had called me out of the blue. It had been years since we were in college together. The last time I'd seen Rob we were drinking coffee and eating donuts, trying not to spill anything on our senior theses. *Why is he calling me now?* I'd wondered. After playing phone tag all week, we had finally connected.

"What happened in your meeting that made it so incredible?" I asked, digging for more details.

"I met with a man in town who owns a local restaurant," he boomed.

Okay. I was expecting something a little more spectacular—like he just landed a new contract for his business, or that he had been diagnosed with cancer and his doctor just told him that his scans were clean. A meeting with a local restaurant owner?

"We were having a cup of coffee together," Rob rushed on, his excitement evident. "Somehow we got talking about our spiritual lives, and the guy began sharing what had happened during his early morning prayer time at the restaurant. God had 'nudged' him to go across the street and meet the owner of another restaurant—his competitor."

Rob stopped for a moment and chuckled, but then he sprinted on with his story. "Like most of us, Bruce, he fought the nudge, because the restaurant owner across the street was stealing business from him—at least that's what he thought. Why in the world would God want him to walk across the road?"

I reflected for a moment. *What would I do in a similar situation?* I'm usually wrapped up in my own busy world, loving those who love me first. I often fail to take the initiative to reach beyond my own circle of friends, especially if of all things it involves someone who might threaten my prosperity. I probably would have repressed the nudge.

"So my friend finally capitulates and walks across the street to meet the competition. Needless to say, the man was shocked and surprised. It's not every day that one's adversary pays an unannounced visit. But his competitor welcomed him, offered him some spice tea, and engaged in a conversation that lasted for a couple of hours."

"In the course of their conversation," said Rob, "my friend discovered that the owner was an Iraqi and his restaurant was really struggling financially. The bank was on his back, foreclosure was possible, and there was a good chance he would lose the business."

Rob became more animated. "Do you know what my friend did when he got back to his restaurant? He gathered his employees together and told them about the dire situation of the owner across the street. On their own initiative the employees took up a collection!"

Rob continued to relate how the two strangers deepened their friendship. Questions about business turned to conversations about family and countries. Questions about family turned to conversations about faith, customs, and traditions. Interestingly, as the men's friendship deepened, business picked up for the man across the street. The banks backed off and the man's livelihood was saved.

Rob's story of this road-crossing Christian sparked a thought. What makes a business truly Christian? I think it has nothing to do with a listing in the Christian Yellow Pages and everything to do with whether or not the business embodies the life and teachings of Jesus in its day-to-day operations. A restaurant owner who embraces his competitor and champions this stranger's cause at the potential expense of his own business exhibits *radical* behavior. In a world most often looking out for its own interests, such self-sacrifice manifests the spirit of the gospel whose center is the Cross.

ROAD MARKER

Sometimes we have to cross the road and check
on the welfare of our competitors.

Rob's story reminded me of Jesus' story about a man throwing a banquet and inviting those who could not pay him back. "Invite *them*," Jesus raised his voice to his listeners. In this one statement Jesus reversed the entire principle of how the social world works—especially in business. Help those who can help us back? Sure, that makes sense. Pharmaceutical companies routinely court doctors by offering free cruises and five-star dinners. The physicians then prescribe those manufacturers' drugs. Company salespeople entice clients with rounds of golf and skybox tickets at the ballpark, expecting product allegiance in return. Nonprofits invite their VIPs to wine and cheese parties, hoping that big donations will follow. I'm not saying that these activities are inherently wrong. But Jesus communicates another message, a message that often gets lost in our pursuit of success and the embrace of our culture.

The story of Rob's friend forces us to ask the question, how many of us would cross the road to embrace our *competition*?

Whether we run a restaurant, an accounting firm, or a health club, would we have the courage and faith to engage in the kind of road-crossing activity displayed by Rob's friend?

In that one embrace, an authentic, radical expression of God's love was communicated to someone who was not expecting it. That is the power of crossing roads. It goes against human convention yet provides the world with a glimpse of another reality—a divine reality. No words are necessary.

A PASTOR: OFFERING UP LIVING KOOL-AID

> *Disinherited people . . . are bleeding to death from*
> *deep social and economic wounds. They need brigades*
> *of ambulance drivers who will have to ignore the red*
> *lights of the present system until the emergency is solved.*
>
> MARTIN LUTHER KING JR.

Maria Edmonds is a pastor in a small town in the mountains of North Carolina. She crossed a road one day . . . and it changed everything.

In her community the proliferation of gang activity was becoming a problem. The community's response to the gangs' presence within the community was fairly typical—fear, demonization ("Those no-good, mannerless kids"), suspicion, and avoidance at all costs. As one writer puts it, "There are few images in our culture more frightening than that of the gang member: tattooed, armed, as likely to shoot you as look at you."[1] Their thinking was, *If we stay on our side of the road, and they stay on theirs, we'll all be fine.*

One Sunday, an edgy teenager named Robin showed up at Maria Edmonds's church. Robin was involved in a skateboarding gang called Toxic. When Robin's initial visit to church turned into more visits (though not every Sunday), Pastor Maria got an idea. She knew that skateboarding gangs were a problem that both the police and nervous residents in the community wanted to go away. She had heard comments—"Where are the parents of those out-of-control kids?"—and Robin had told her about the police harassing him and his friends.

Compelled by her faith in a road-crossing Jesus, Pastor Maria started visiting the skaters' hangout. She never arrived at the skating pit empty handed. But she wasn't carrying a Bible or a flyer highlighting the next church activity. In her hand she toted an insulated jug of well-iced grape, sometimes strawberry, Kool-Aid! She knew that even leather-tough skateboarding kids got thirsty. After a while, the skaters looked forward to her "pastoral calls," especially since she always seemed to arrive at the hottest, most humid moment of the day. This went on for weeks.

One especially torrid afternoon, Pastor Maria arrived at the skating pit and heard the news: Robin had died. None of the boys knew the details of exactly how it happened. "Some mysterious cause," one skater said. Pastor Maria tracked down Robin's parents, because she had a plan.

The moment she heard about Robin, Pastor Maria knew that she wanted to hold a special memorial service for Robin and his skateboarding friends. She purchased *the* skateboard that Robin had on layaway at Kmart. Pastor Maria placed the brand-new, glistening board on the altar at the front of her church and invited the skate gang to come and write farewell messages on the board. A hundred kids showed up at the service. Some of them told their stories and remembered their friend Robin.

It was the first time that most of the young toughs had ever been inside a church, which was a good enough reason for Pastor Maria to take some theological liberties with her message. She likened heaven to a skatepark. For some of us, the thought of loud sounds of metal scraping against concrete curbs and sidewalks is not our idea of eternal bliss. Nowhere in the book of Revelation does it describe heaven as being filled with teens doing kickflips down the twenty-four-karat gold streets. But that's how Pastor Maria's message began that morning. Her skateboard imagery made perfect sense to Robin's buddies in the audience.

In memory of Robin, the pastor suggested to her congregation that the church build a place where the kids could gather and skate safely. She knew full well that there would be members who would not think it was a worthy church capital campaign. A *skate ramp* in their parking lot? Get serious.

Yet the road-crossing activity of Pastor Maria infected her congregation with a road-crossing vision. Edmonds had crossed the road first with a cold cup of Kool-Aid . . . and her people followed. The power and significance of crossing roads is when people see the possibilities and everyone decides to join the journey.

Pastor Maria's skate ramps were built, a member of the church who was an insurance broker wrote a policy, and a ministry called The Walk was birthed. The skaters were really excited about their coolest-of-cool ramps. So the obvious next step was to create exciting new programs for the youth: tutoring, Bible studies, skateboard blessings, and job-search assistance. Skateboards, which formerly had been scrawled with profanity, now had Bible verses etched in bright colors.

ROAD MARKER

Sometimes we have to cross the road and enjoy
skateboarders in the church parking lot.

Maria Edmonds and her congregation offered the growing crowd of kids love "without strings attached."[2] They had discovered that when kids don't feel welcome at a church, they create their own "societies of welcome." (Sadly, when those negative "societies of welcome" outside the church open their arms to alienated young people, those who join have sad and often devastating consequences.)

Thankfully, Pastor Maria's church was different.

What inspires a congregation to build a skatepark or implement another innovative program? Why would a church group reach out to those who live different lives on the fringes of society? It always begins when a group of God's people have their eyes and minds and hearts opened to exciting possibilities.

And how were the eyes and minds and hearts of God's people in Pastor Maria's church opened? With electric guitars and drums in the sanctuary for Sunday-morning worship? No. Cutting-edge preaching? No. More weekly Bible studies? No. When Maria Edmonds crossed the road and beckoned her congregation to follow, her parishioners grew in their faith. And when the faith of her parishioners expanded, it made room in their hearts for strangers.

Because of one congregation's step of faith in crossing the road, former gang members and skateboarders in a small North Carolina town are now eternally refreshed by living waters. Sure, those kids still like a gulp of chilled Kool-Aid on a hot day, but the drink that satisfies their youthful restlessness is the "water" of a loving embrace that they experience each time they are welcomed by Christ's followers.

A LAWYER: GUESS WHO'S COMING FOR DINNER?

We do not think ourselves into a new way of living,
we live ourselves into a new way of thinking.

RICHARD ROHR[3]

"I'm such a bad example," confessed Jay. "I was no more than two minutes off the seminary campus when I cursed at a driver who cut in front of me. I'm going to have to clean up my act."

I have always appreciated this one fact about my friend Jay—there is not a more honest, candid person on the face of this earth. Jay is Jay. What you see is what you get. No pretense. Real.

Still, I wasn't expecting the curveball he threw at me: Jay, 52, enrolled in a three-year master's in theology program. It wasn't like he needed something to do. He had a thriving law practice, four kids, and a wonderful wife, and was active in his church and a trustee on multiple organizations' boards.

"Of all things, Jay, why are you going to seminary?" I asked, expecting to hear something like "I really feel God is calling me" or "I want to enrich my understanding of the Christian faith."

His answer surprised me. "I could give you some lofty explanation, but I think it's kind of an ego thing. It sure is fun talking about stuff like eschatology and Christian apologetics. Previously my three favorite things were (1) sex, (2) golf, and (3) hunting. Seminary is now number two." I smiled. It confirmed my notion: Jay was about to break the mold of your typical seminary student.

So why did I get a call on the evening of Jay's first day at seminary, after Jay had flipped off the guy that cut in front of his car? Because Jay couldn't wait to share what had happened on his first day. He was like a kid blown away by how good kindergarten was—his enthusiasm was infectious.

First, there was the paper notepad thing. "Can you believe it? I couldn't buy a pad of paper at the bookstore!" he said, still reeling from the shock of it all. It was a far cry from his days at law school; notepads had been replaced by laptops as the preferred note-taking device. And the students weren't all taking notes on what the professor was saying. "The guy in front of me was shopping online for lakeshore rentals in the Poconos during the lecture on the theory of the end times! Things have really changed!"

Then there was Jay's encounter with a twenty-year-old student. Jay had arrived early for his hermeneutics class to catch up on his reading. He was sitting at the back of the class, in his white button-down oxford shirt, maroon tie, and sport jacket.

"The kid looked at me and said, 'Excuse me, sir, are you teaching from the back of the class today?'" Jay let out one of his great laughs.

But then Jay became serious. "You know, Bruce, an interesting thing happened after class at lunch. I came out of the serving line with tray in hand and immediately noticed the dynamics of how people were seated in the room. Sure enough, the Korean students were sitting together; the women were sitting together; the Latinos were at another table. Off in the corner were the African American students. The white students sat closest to the serving line.

"I thought the configuration of racial groupings was curious, maybe depressing, especially for a seminary campus," Jay said. "So you know me, I decided to try a little experiment. I sat by myself. I wanted to see who might come and sit with the older man in the starched white oxford shirt and maroon tie. But then I decided to abort my experiment. I stepped out of my comfort zone and headed to the table with the African American students."

I have grown to love Jay's politically incorrect candor, and as he went on, I wasn't disappointed. "You know, I'm the stereotypical white guy. I barely know three black people in history—Martin Luther King Jr. is one of them. So I'm thinking to myself, *What are these guys going to think when I crash their party? Will they talk with me? Do they have an ax to grind?* Better that I find out sooner, rather than later. One thing I knew for sure, I was way out of my comfort zone."

As an estate lawyer, Jay's public contacts were limited to his own social circles that didn't include a cluster of African American seminarians. It was a big step for Jay to be back in school. Now he was challenging the unspoken borders in a seminary dining room.

As Jay walked toward the table, balancing his club soda and

chicken salad on a tray, he heard one of the students say, "I can't believe it, guys, we've done it again—we've just perpetuated the stereotype by sitting together."

Jay was laughing in the phone at this point. "Bruce, my friend, my timing could not have been better. I slammed down my tray and said with a smile, 'Your problem has just been solved.' For a split second those guys gave me a shocked look, then we all broke up laughing."

That lunchtime, friendships were formed when Jay stepped into a whole new world.

ROAD MARKER

Sometimes we have to cross the road and have
lunch with a table full of strangers.

So what's the big deal? A middle-aged white guy decides to get out of his comfort zone and break bread with a group of African American students? Was the issue of race relations really furthered that day? Maybe not. But a road was crossed that afternoon. Those future church leaders, training to be shapers of the body of Christ, were startled to recognize that they were still isolated by barriers. It took a middle-aged white guy, who attended class one day a week, to jar them from their complicity of keeping safe within their own racial groupings.

As an outsider to the road-crossing adventure, Jay was struck that our future church leaders flocked together like birds of a feather. Granted, this was one lunch, and perhaps it did not represent ongoing "clustering" patterns of seminary students, but it doesn't surprise me.

As I speak at different churches across the country, I am amazed at the segregation of our congregations. Is the lack of integration linked to the lack of a road-crossing vision on the part of our church leaders? When our leaders do not embrace the road-crossing nature of Jesus' life as a spiritual discipline, is it surprising that our congregations are homogeneous, one-dimensional places? Paul wonderfully provided a theological foundation for the church when he reminded his readers that "there is neither Jew nor Greek, slave nor free, male nor female, for you are all one in Christ Jesus" (Galatians 3:28).

To fulfill Paul's vision for the church it takes leadership that celebrates our oneness and challenges the barriers that divide us. Road crossing takes work, it takes vision, and it takes the belief that it is a critical component of healthy spiritual growth for a church to reflect the richness and diversity of humanity.

We can all relate to Jay in some way. Standing with our trays of food, surveying the tables in the cafeteria, and wondering with whom to sit is a metaphor of life that we can all embrace. Will we choose the comfortable solution or will we cross the road?

A VETERINARIAN:
I DIDN'T WANT TO COME THIS WEEKEND

> *How beautiful are the feet of those*
> *who bring good news!*
>
> ROMANS 10:15

Bob is an impressive veterinarian with a thriving practice. He spends most of his time lovingly patching up cats and dogs, but in his spare time he explores God's beautiful creation. He hikes, canoes, or kayaks every weekend he can. For Bob, sitting on the top of a mountain vista with a handful of trail mix and being dazzled by an orange and rust sunset is way better than anything you can find on TV.

Years ago, Bob started volunteering with one of our ministry's programs called UrbanTrekkers.[4] The trekkers, inner-city teenagers, undergo an expeditional learning opportunity. The group has traveled to the Pacific Northwest, canoed through the New Jersey Pine Barrens, climbed Mt. Washington in New Hampshire, explored the Florida Everglades, and skated in New York City's Central Park. On each of the adventures the students learn about the environment and indigenous history, perform acts of community service, and experience cross-cultural learning. Over the years, Bob has admitted that he's not really a youth guy, but interacting with the kids has changed his life.

"How was your recent trip?" I asked him. The group had just returned from a four-day trip to Maine, where they met up with a group of other impoverished students; most of them work on and maintain the lobster boats with their parents. Most people assume that the entire state of Maine is wealthy. What the summer tourists don't see is how severe the rural poverty in Maine really is.

A big grin creased Bob's face. "That trip was remarkable; the last night was something I'll never forget."

"Tell me about it!"

"Our Camden kids had just made a 'Philadelphia meal' for the Maine students. Sharika and Ebony created the most delicious cheesesteaks; Jim had brought some fresh Jersey corn on the cob (it's the best in the world). We finished dinner and cleaned up the dishes. Sitting around the campfire, the kids began to talk about the significance of the weekend.

"One of the boys from Maine, a skinny, acne-pocked white kid, looked at our group and said with his unique down east brogue, 'Ya know, I wasn't gonna come on this trip when I discovered we were going to be hanging out with a bunch of black kids. I was about to cancel. Now I'm glad I was here and just want to thank ya for coming. I learned a lot this weekend.'"

Bob looked at me, obviously touched by the honesty of that confession. "That was a pretty gutsy thing for that quiet kid to say. But that was just the beginning.

"Another kid raised his hand. 'My dad's a racist. If he knew

I was here with you this weekend, he'd beat me. I don't know how I'm gonna face him. All I've learned about people of different races is what he taught me. And that's to hate. Now I'm thinking different. You guys have been great and taught me a lot. Thanks.'

"For the rest of the night the kids just shared about their lives, where they lived, and what kinds of pressures they dealt with on a daily basis. African American and Puerto Rican kids from the inner city eagerly talked with the kids from rural Maine into the wee hours of the morning, learning about one another and growing in understanding. It was magic. One of God's smiling miracles."

The kids returned from that trip, Bob told me, realizing there are different kinds of poverty not relegated to our urban communities. There are problems in rural America too. Drugs, alcohol abuse, and dysfunctional families exist everywhere. But the kids did not just learn about shared problems; they also learned about shared opportunities—opportunities to return home and challenge the views of their parents and adult authorities who hold bigoted views.

ROAD MARKER

Sometimes we have to cross the road to discover
that our ideas about people can change.

Imagine if there were a thousand adults like Bob across this country, committed to creating "campfire experiences" for young people from different races, classes, and environments. That would translate into thousands of young people engaging in the disciplines of road crossing, experiencing the wonders of an expanded worldview, diminishing fear of others, and creating the capacity for a younger generation of truly compassionate people.

Bob may not consider himself to be a youth guy, but he was a different man after his trip to Maine. The honesty of the youth, their willingness to discuss significant issues, their confessions, and their eagerness to return home and make a difference made Bob a believer of road-crossing Christianity. Bob realized that the prophet Isaiah was on target when he claimed that a "child will lead them" (11:6).

STARTING A MOVEMENT

The truisms that a tidal wave begins with a ripple, a raging river with hundreds of small tributaries, and a forest fire with a small spark can't be argued. Why should it be any different with a social or religious movement? Great historic, cultural, and sociological changes—movements for civil rights, women's rights, or children's rights—usually begin with a single person who is willing to think differently. And when this thinking leads to action, others begin to follow; our neighborhoods, our churches, and our country begin to change.

A pastor in North Carolina, a restaurant owner in Colorado, a part-time seminary student, and a veterinarian who loves to backpack have given us reason to embrace a new kind of Christian discipline, a discipline that transforms its participants. It is the discipline of road crossing. Let's join these friends or, better yet, start our own movement!

THE HEART OF THE TRAVEL ITINERARY

It is God who says, "Behold, I create all things new."
Therefore God's most persistent enemies must be those
who are unwilling to move in new directions. . . .
If you choose, you're sometimes wrong; but if
you never choose, you're always wrong.

WILLIAM SLOANE COFFIN[1]

A few years ago, I was reminded of the importance of commitment to a road-crossing lifestyle. I was invited to a glitzy reception where my son was to be awarded a five-year financial aid scholarship to a private grade school. Showing up was the least I could do, but I confess that I am an introvert by nature. Thus, shuffling between clusters of adults who were discussing football, the new fifth-grade teacher, and the township politics was, to put it mildly, agonizing.

After an awkward and unsuccessful attempt to break into a huddle of soccer dads, I decided to migrate toward the vegetable tray. Like a nervous rabbit, I chewed on a celery stick and became fully conscious of my isolation. I glanced at my watch for the third time: another thirty-seven minutes before the principal's address. After that, I would unobtrusively disappear.

A mother, Joan, approached the buffet. I knew Joan from other back-to-school nights. The last time we had run into each other, we had talked excitedly about the possibility of her returning to seminary to work on an advanced degree in theology.

"Hi, Joan," I said. "Did you ever go to seminary?" Joan looked a little startled as she bit hard on a carrot stick. Having someone ask her about seminary at a cocktail party was probably the last thing she ever expected. After all, religion and politics are topics to avoid if one wants an amicable evening of idle chitchat.

Before long we were engaged in a rather in-depth conversation, discussing differences between various faith traditions. When I glanced again at my watch, I had burned eighteen minutes and felt better about making it through the evening.

"Tell me a little about *your* work," Joan said, smiling. I smiled back, feeling awkward, but knew that my answer was going to take at least twenty minutes. I launched into a detailed description of our work in the inner city, of the urban crises, and the kids whose dreams get crushed from their grindingly difficult environment. I stopped and took a breath.

She chimed in. "*My* most vivid childhood memory from the late sixties is sitting on the rooftop of my Newark home—watching the city burn while the National Guard combed the streets with machine guns."

I never would have guessed that this fully adapted suburban woman was a city kid.

She remembered vividly watching the racial unrest of that time sweeping the land while urban America was going up in flames. Watts. Detroit. Chicago. Washington. Tulsa. Pittsburgh. Atlantic City. But Newark was the worst. Many deaths. And millions of dollars in damages from riots starting after an erroneous report flashed through the town that a black cabdriver had been arrested and beaten.

"Police sealed the city. There were checkpoints at each of the entryways. No one could get in or out without a security escort. Worse, my parents were away when things began to break loose, so they called my grandfather to get me out of the city. But Grandpa wouldn't."

Strange behavior on the part of a grandfather, I thought. "Why didn't he listen to the police and get you out of there?"

"He was German," she said bluntly. "*His* family had fled Germany in the late 1930s because of the Nazis, but he felt guilty about that the remainder of his life." Joan paused, looking at me intently. "'When good people run, evil triumphs,' recited my grandfather, as if this line had haunted him for years."

She continued, her emotions welling. "Newark was going up in flames, and I have never forgotten his words. He was not going to run a second time. He was not about to pull up stakes when the going got tough. From his own childhood he knew the corroding consequences of running in the face of hardship."

Joan said that her grandfather had lived his life with regret even though it was his family that had made the decision to run from the Nazi regime. But wedged between his feelings of guilt was a profound truth—*evil grows where it is not engaged and resisted.* Evil things happen when there are no voices or lives to stand in opposition. Where good people do nothing—not confronting lies, not promoting reconciliation, not standing with the demonized, not building relationships—the bad guys win.

The simple, profound equation: *when good people run, evil triumphs.*

It still happens today. Why does one person's faith aggressively compel him or her to move *toward* a problem and cross roads—standing courageously, embracing change, fighting for justice, understanding opposition, loving the enemy—whereas another person's faith calls him or her to run toward safety and stay in a protective realm? Both people run. They just run in different directions, and that makes all the difference.

Part of the answer, it seems to me, is found in the way we think about our faith, the way we interpret the call of the gospel in our lives. I strongly believe that our Christian faith is about moving beyond our primal, self-preserving impulses and actively looking for ways to expand our relational circles so we can learn, grow, and share the gifts God has bestowed upon our lives.

ROAD MARKER

Jesus crossed the road to bring the Good News
of his saving grace to all people.

The teachings of Jesus proclaim that the authentic follower is someone whose life will grow in its complexity and difficulty because of his or her commitments and choices. The life of Jesus reveals a man who was willing to cross all kinds of roads in an effort to bring his liberating news of a loving God, an awesome grace, and a healing power.

No. It's not time to run away. It *is* time (past time) to courageously add road crossing to our list of spiritual disciplines. We will change because of our commitment; our world will too.

BACK TO BASICS

I admire a man named Bob Lupton. I do not know him personally, but I respect his ministry. For over thirty years he has worked in some of Atlanta's most dangerous and difficult communities, transforming them into places of peace and prosperity. He is a minister in the truest sense, not only caring for the souls of people, but also caring about the social issues that impact their lives. Bob is also one of the great practical urban theologians—possessing a remarkable ability to integrate theological truth with the gritty realities of urban life. Bob has never run away from difficult circumstances.

Instead, Bob has run toward the evils of poverty and societal neglect, embraced those problems with courage and commitment, and helped develop creative solutions. Whole communities have been transformed because of his efforts. His life personifies the positive transformation that can occur when people cross roads.

A few years ago Bob lectured at a conservative Bible college in the Midwest, a school (we won't mention names) that prides itself on its high view of Scripture and assures its loyal contributors that every student will graduate with a "truly biblical worldview."

Bob posed a question to the class of new freshmen: "Of all the things Jesus commands Christians to do, what is the most important?"

"To evangelize," exclaimed one young man in the front row. "To make disciples," chimed in another. "To get people saved so they can go to heaven," fired off another. "To feed the poor," added one more. "Build the church!" retorted the kid in the back of the class.

The class was quite proud of its biblically informed answers. This was no liberal, wayward college; it was a conservative Christian college that had remained faithful to its roots.

"I'm surprised," began Bob with a soft rebuke. "This is a Bible college, and yet nobody knows what the most important command of Jesus is?" Bob looked at the audience. They weren't pleased with Bob's rebuke. To question their biblical knowledge was an affront to their sensibilities. "Come on," he beckoned. "What does the Bible *actually* say is the most important thing we can do?"

A student who had a black leather, gold-embossed Bible open on his desk gave a how-could-I-have-missed-it look and yelled, "To preach the Good News!"

Bob shook his head, paused momentarily, and then cleared his throat. "You're all wrong!" Silence. Looks of bewilderment. Who was this freak liberal? "At least, according to the Gospel writers— if you're interested in what *they* have to say," teased Bob. "In the twelfth chapter of Mark, Jesus reminds his listening audience that the supreme command is, Love the Lord your God with all your heart, soul, strength, and mind. And love your neighbor as yourself" (verses 30-31).

Bob probably should have stopped there—that is, if he wanted an invitation to return again, but he decided to push his point a little further.

"I wonder how biblical this college really is?" he continued to press. "As I look through the curriculum I am surprised that there are no courses being taught on loving one's neighbor. There is no 'Neighbor Love 101' or 'Understanding Your Neighbor in a Modern World.' Or how about 'Neighborly Love in a Cross-Cultural Context.' Nothing! I see courses on everything else— eschatology, systematics, hermeneutics—but there's *nothing* on loving one's neighbor."

By this time Bob was beginning to, how should I say it, *feel the Spirit*. And the freshmen saints were getting a holy spanking. Bob was on a roll.

"If loving God and loving neighbor is the most important mandate of our faith," Bob concluded, "then coursework on applying this teaching to practice should be a major emphasis of a college committed to preparing Christian leaders."

I am not sure what happened to Bob after class that day. He did not share that part in his monthly newsletter. I can only imagine that he might have been escorted off the campus, shielded from rotten tomatoes hurled by disgruntled students.

But Bob's point was profound.

Bob's dismayed classroom reminds us of what Jesus made so clear and so simple. Jesus reduced the essence of Christian behavior down to a pithy statement—love God, love neighbor. According to Jesus, the rest is background music. And yet how often does the background music become the solo performance, distracting us from what really matters?

ROAD MARKER

Sometimes we have to cross the road to
be the neighbor God wants us to be.

We read titillating books about the end times, endlessly debate whether we are post- or premillennialist, split churches over methods of baptism, and write endless tomes on the problems of evil. Ironically there is little time spent debating the implications and strategies for loving neighbors and the challenges that presents. I've never heard of a church splitting over the best practices of neighborly love. Instead, we fight about maintaining stained glass windows or what color the carpet in the sanctuary should be.

NEIGHBORLY LOVE

When Jesus reduced the faith down to two easy-to-remember commands, he made the bold claim that we are to love those who live outside the four walls of our home. However we want to define *neighbor*, most of us agree that neighbors include people who live outside our most immediate social circles. For most of us, actually loving a neighbor would mean crossing some kind of road, barrier, border, divide, street, or fence—physical, psychological, or social. Loving our neighbors means getting out of our comfort zones, our gated communities, and our homogeneous neighborhoods and reaching out to the broader world community. Neighborly love, by its very definition, implies some kind of road-crossing activity.

Perhaps the reason Jesus made neighbor love one of the two greatest of all commands is that, if exercised, its impact would be transformative to both those who practice it and those who receive it.

It is hardly accidental that Jesus illustrated the command to love one's neighbor with one of the most radical road-crossing stories in the New Testament—the story of the Good Samaritan. No doubt the Jewish listeners would have been shocked by the implications of a Samaritan crossing a road to tend to the wounds of their Jewish brother. Remember, these two groups of people despised each other. The image produces a disorienting dilemma for the listener and pushes him or her beyond that which is comfortable. Jesus clearly articulated a whole new realm of what it means to love and receive love. In the story of the Good Samaritan all participants are changed—the giver, the receiver, and the observer. That is what road-crossing love does.

FOR SUCH A TIME AS THIS

Curiously, in the immediate wake of the devastating 9/11 attacks on the World Trade Center Twin Towers and a wing of the Pentagon, the number of racially motivated hate crimes dramatically increased. Arabs who lived peaceably in our country for years—paying taxes, holding jobs, being involved in civic and community activities—were now viewed suspiciously because of their dress, ethnicity, and religion. Neighbors who formerly greeted one another with smiles and handshakes now viewed each other with contempt and suspicion. After all, it could be possible that the Muslim family at the end of the block were terrorists. And the Pakistani family living next door? I suppose they could mail out letters filled with anthrax. That was how too many of us thought. If you were a person of Middle Eastern descent, it was not a great time to live in America.

Should this behavior surprise us? Not when fear is in the air. Most humans revert to their most base human instinct—survive at all costs. Transferring our fear onto unsuspecting people—through scapegoating, name-calling, joke telling, and slander—is behavior that can instinctively take control.

I would like to believe that in times of crisis and heightened fear, Christians act markedly different from the rest of the population. I would like to believe that the years we spend cultivating our faith, embracing the teachings of Jesus, walking in the Spirit, and dying to self would impact the way we react at such times. Sadly, I do not think that is always the case.

So post-9/11 in what some call a Christian nation, we read about cases of harassment, vandalism of people's homes and property, and graffiti on the walls of mosques. People became afraid to come out of their houses, children were afraid to go to school, parents were afraid to go shopping.

ROAD MARKER

Sometimes we have to cross the road to
celebrate God's diversity of humanity.

But during that time I remember reading a powerful story about a group of Presbyterian women. They were just ordinary women—no advanced degrees in intercultural studies, no specialized training in cross-cultural ministry. Just a group of stay-at-home moms who were dismayed and saddened by the visible manifestations of hostility they saw in their neighborhoods. I cannot recall where they lived. I do not remember the church. But the story jumped off the page of the newspaper because it so vividly portrayed the spirit of Christian faith.

Troubled, this group of women started knocking on the doors of Muslim homes in their community, inviting the women, in neighborly fashion, just to go shopping. Shopping is a pretty universal activity—a necessity for some, a sport for others. The women did not come to convert their neighbors or invite them to church. In the words of Volf, they came with their arms wide open and with a willingness to wait. Needless to say, the Muslim women were amazed at the display of hospitality and neighborly love. And for months these women from different traditions continued to deepen their friendships as they shopped together on a weekly basis. In the presence of the Presbyterian women, the Muslim sisters felt safe. Also I am sure that the faith and lives of both groups were enriched and broadened.

To me this was yet another example of road crossing. In a time when our world thirsts for authentic expressions of Christian faith, it is refreshing to hear stories of people who confront their fears, who suspend their judgments, and who courageously walk to the other side and embrace their neighbors. This is the pattern of Jesus' life. This is a repetitive activity reflecting a discipline, a practice, a regular expression of his faith in the world. To those carrying his name today, Jesus calls out and reminds us to rediscover the often overlooked discipline of road crossing. With this challenge comes a promise: Our faith journey will be enriched. Our lives will be transformed. And our world will be changed.

DISCUSSION QUESTIONS
FOR YOUR JOURNEY

Introduction: Open the Eyes of My Heart

When is the last time you really changed a perspective, a habit, or an attitude? What instigated the change?

What does road crossing mean to you? Have you ever thought about it as a spiritual discipline?

What is the last significant road (boundary, barrier, border) you crossed? In what ways did the experience impact your life and your faith?

Chapter One: Where Did Jesus Travel?

When you think about Jesus crossing roads, barriers, and boundaries, what situations come to mind? Do you think he crossed these roads intentionally?

What is the purpose of a spiritual discipline?

Do you agree that traditional spiritual disciplines can simply reinforce what we want to believe and allow us to remain unchanged? If so, why? If not, why not?

Why do so many people see borders as impenetrable barriers—rather than places of encounter and exchange?

Chapter Two: Welcoming Disorienting Dilemmas

Why are disorienting dilemmas so critical for initiating true change?

In what ways does Jesus create "disorienting dilemmas" for his disciples and listeners? Share some concrete examples of where Jesus uses this tactic to jolt his disciples towards change.

What does a spiritually mature person look like to you? Who is someone who represents a spiritually mature person?

Why does Ronald Marstin argue that spiritual maturity implies a "broadening" of social relations? Do you agree?

Chapter Three: Can a Rock Really Change?

Do you know someone you like to banter with over issues of theology? If so, what is the hot topic that gets you passionate? Why is that topic important to you?

Can you share a situation where a firmly held conviction was changed because of a relationship with another human being? What was it about that relationship that provoked you to change?

Peter's story is fascinating. Why do you think God uses an encounter with a Gentile to broaden Peter's understanding of God's grace?

Nicholas Wolterstorff experienced change by "hearing the voices" and "seeing the faces" of those who had experienced oppression and hardship. What voices do you need to hear? What faces do you need to see?

Chapter Four: Crossing the Road to the Poor

"We see from where we stand," claims the Haitian proverb. Have you ever "stood" in a poor community, listening to stories, learning its history, and watching the faces? Describe the experience. What kind of impact did it have on you?

As Christians, why is it crucial to understand the perspective of poor people?

Why is Jesus' question to Bartimaeus so critical? What does that question reveal about the spirit of road crossing?

How might you cross a road to the poor this week or this month? What questions might you ask?

Chapter Five: Crossing the Road of Race

Do you think Joel Cartwright's attempt to diversify his Christmas party was a worthy attempt at creating a conversation about race and difference? If not, why not?

What would be the equivalent of wandering through Samaritan territory today? What is the Samaria in your life?

The Presbyterian Prayer of Confession reads: "Loving God, we admit to attitudes that exclude rather than embrace. We prefer to associate with others who think and act as we do. We turn away from those who are different from us. We identify some as enemies to be avoided or even destroyed. Forgive us, God, for seeking to limit your family." What does this prayer mean to you? How is it that people can recite this prayer of confession, year after year, and never act upon its basic premise?

Do you think racism is still a problem in our country? What is the best way to deal with prejudice?

Chapter Six: Crossing the Road of Spiritual Exclusivity

How do you think your congregation would respond if a foulmouthed stripper walked into the sanctuary on a Sunday morning?

Why does Jesus seem so free from the expectations of other people—especially religious leaders like those we often seek to please?

How do Christians best live in this tension between holding "standards" and ensuring that people who do not meet those standards still feel accepted and loved?

Who are some of the "spiritually inappropriate" people you might engage? What might that engagement cost you in terms of your reputation?

Chapter Seven: Crossing the Road to Our Enemies

Have you ever intentionally loved an enemy? If so, what did you do? What happened? What impact did it have on your life?

Do you believe that our enemies can be more like us than different? What creates enemies? How might road crossing dismantle enemy-creating agents?

If loving our enemies is not optional for the Christian, then why do we find it so difficult? Why do we choose not to obey?

The mandatum that Richard John Neuhaus describes is a kind of love that is not "of our desiring," but a "demanding love." Are there different kinds of love? Would you be able to wash the feet of a friend who you knew was going to betray you? Why or why not?

Chapter Eight: Crossing the Road of Cultural Worldview

Is it difficult for you to talk politics with someone who votes differently from you? Why? Do you make moral and spiritual judgments about their politics?

What might be a modern-day equivalent to Jesus' responding to the Roman centurion's request for help? Who represents the centurion in your life?

Is it important to seek out those who hold a different worldview than our own? If so, why? If not, why not?

Why do you think Jesus upheld this centurion as a model of faith? What can we learn from his testimony? Do you think it is possible that some of our best examples of faith might come from the most unexpected people? Have you ever experienced this?

Have you ever engaged with a person of another faith? Why is it important for Christians to dialogue with those of other faiths?

What can Lee Atwater's deathbed confession teach us about alienating and maligning brothers and sisters on the basis of their political convictions?

Chapter Nine: The Roadblock of Fear

Can you identify with those who are afraid of poor, urban communities? What fuels that fear? What can you do to eliminate that fear?

Do you believe fear is part of our biological makeup? How do you think we can best overcome the fear of the other?

What does the biblical command "fear not" mean to you? How could it be applied in your own life?

Can you identify with Moses' fear of confronting Pharaoh? How might you have reacted?

What do you think Moses learned from "going to hell" that he would not have learned had he stayed in the desert? How do you think his faith changed?

Chapter Ten: The Roadblock of Indifference

Why does Elie Wiesel believe that indifference is the great enemy? Do you agree?

How can road crossing move Christians beyond indifference?

What are some of the dangers of becoming a truly compassionate person?

How does the lavish gift of Brent sharing his Christmas bonus illustrate how relationships can pull us out of a state of indifference?

Chapter Eleven: The Roadblock of Misguided Theology

What is your understanding of the blessed life? How does your understanding of blessing align itself with Jesus' idea as presented in the Beatitudes?

How can we, as Christians, make sense of the tension between the Old Testament notion of blessing and Jesus' notion?

Why do the things we often associate with blessing—wealth, good food, laughter, esteem from our friends—all make it onto Jesus' "woe" list? Is Jesus just a killjoy, or is there a spiritual truth we need to learn from his perspective?

Jesus never preaches a gospel of otherworldliness. The gospel Jesus preaches is about engaging in the here and now. Why do Christians continually want a faith that seeks to disengage them from the harsh realities of life?

The Old Testament prophets' and Jesus' understanding of worship seem to differ radically from that of many contemporary Christian churches. Why is this the case? What can be done?

Examine the words of your favorite worship songs. What kind of theology do they suggest? Do the songs encourage disengagement from the world?

Chapter Twelve: Second-Floor Christianity and the Art of Embrace

When was the last time you got to the "second floor"—that place beyond the surface of a situation—and really saw what was taking place? How did you get there? How did you build enough trust?

Think about a road you need to cross—a road of race, geography, ideology, socioeconomics, ethnicity. What would opening your arms look like? What would waiting look like? What would an embrace look like?

Using Volf's model of embrace, how might you apply the four stages to a situation in your life?

How can you decenter yourself this week and make space for that person on the other side of the road?

Chapter Thirteen: Road-Crossing Adventures: A Businessman, a Pastor, a Lawyer, and a Veterinarian

Jesus called his disciples to get into their boat and travel to the "other side." What might the "other side" look like for you this week?

How might you apply Volf's stages of embrace to our four road crossers: How did they open their arms and make space for the other? How did they wait? How did they embrace? How did they let go and leave with traces of the other?

What can you learn from each of these road crossers that can be applied to your own life?

What was the impact on the spiritual growth of those in the stories who crossed roads?

What was the impact on those who witnessed and experienced the act of the road crossers?

Conclusion: The Heart of the Travel Itinerary

Why is it so hard for us, like the students at the Bible college, to stay focused on Jesus' central commands?

In an increasingly "shrinking" world, who is our neighbor? In a country that is increasingly diverse and cosmopolitan, why is it critical to develop the discipline of road crossing?

"When good people run, evil triumphs." In what ways have you been running away from the things and people Jesus wants you to engage?

Outline a road-crossing travel itinerary for the next month. Build in authentic second-floor experiences and border crossings with people who live outside your comfort zone. Reflect on these experiences.

APPENDIX A

OPPORTUNITIES TO CROSS THE ROAD

If *Why Jesus Crossed the Road* inspires you to do more, here are suggestions for how to get involved:

- Explore opportunities at www.urbanpromiseusa.org and www.urbanpromiseinternational.org to see how you can get involved in road-crossing activities with our ministries in Camden, New Jersey; Vancouver, British Columbia; Toronto, Ontario; Wilmington, Delaware; Malawi, Africa; or Honduras, Central America. Each of these programs seeks to equip underserved children and teens with the skills necessary for academic achievement, life management, spiritual growth, and Christian leadership. We incorporate volunteers and missionaries in multiple capacities.
- Suggest *Why Jesus Crossed the Road* to a friend, colleague, book club, Bible study group, church, high school class, or those interested in becoming agents of change in the world.
- Write a *Why Jesus Crossed the Road* book review for Amazon.com, Barnes & Noble, Borders, or Christian Booksellers, or a blog. Your candid comments will help get people interested in this topic of road crossing.
- Share a road-crossing experience with others by visiting www.whyjesuscrossedtheroad.com. We want to inspire other people to see the importance, beauty, and

significance of crossing roads as a regular part of their spiritual disciplines.

- Have Bruce Main come speak at your church or group on this topic or other topics. Book Bruce through visiting www.urbanpromiseusa.org.

For more information contact:
UrbanPromise Ministries
PO Box 1479
Camden, NJ 08107

APPENDIX B

ELABORATING ON A LOVE STORY IN FOUR ACTS

ACT ONE: OPENING OUR ARMS

When we stand face-to-face with an individual we have crossed the road to meet, the first act is symbolically *opening* our arms. Opening our arms might mean inviting someone for a cup of coffee or a meal, or simply placing ourselves in that person's presence. Miroslav Volf claims that this simple gesture sends a message to the other. It is a message of invitation, that is, a "sign that I have *created space* in myself for the other."[1]

In simplistic terms, Volf writes that to truly embrace the other there needs to be a conscious decision to include the other. Just because we cross the road does not mean we have made this conscious decision. We can cross roads yet put up our armor to protect our territory—which is what happened when the inner-city children showed up at the corporate Christmas party and threatened the space of the employees. For a road crossing to turn into a true embrace there needs to be a conscious, authentic decision to make room for the other. Dropping our prejudices, releasing our fears, and checking our egos can all be part of the process.

Most of us already know that making space for *the other* is extremely difficult. But Volf appeals to the apostle Paul and his critical teaching on the significance of the Crucifixion. "I have been crucified with Christ; and it is no longer I who live, but it is Christ who lives in me. And the life I now live in the flesh I live by faith in the Son of God, who loved me and gave himself for me" (Galatians 2:19-20, NRSV). Thus Paul challenges the self-centered life by claiming that left to our own human nature, we gravitate to a wrongly centered self that needs to be "de-centered by being nailed to the cross."[2]

Volf applies the apostle Paul's statement to the act of embracing another: the first movement in truly embracing the person on the other side of the road is coming to the place where we shift from being self-centered to being *other*-centered. When we become other-centered our sense of self is no longer validated in our possessions, our tribes, our races, our jobs, our titles, or our reputations. Instead, as Christians who have been "crucified with Christ," we are free from the limitations and restrictions of these temporal identities. We are released to expand our sense of self—a self that can now include relationships with people our peers and communities might deem unacceptable.

This idea, I believe, is one of the great challenges of authentic Christian faith. As we embrace the reality that our lives have been crucified, and that Christ frees us to become bigger people—people who have created room within our hearts for those who might even challenge us to change and see life from a different perspective—we are liberated to cross roads. Thank goodness Paul, pointedly and happily, reminds us that we do not have to play the games the world offers. Our true identity is found in a crucified Christ who wants us to grow to be people who truly cultivate a heart for all of God's humanity. Whenever we deny the access of the other into our hearts, whenever we fail to create this space, we limit what Jesus did on the cross for humanity.

ACT TWO: WAITING

Volf suggests that after *opening* our arms, the second act of embrace is *waiting*. This act of waiting is critical in the process of a true embrace and an authentic road-crossing experience. Through the opening of arms we initiate a movement toward the stranger, the enemy, or the poor. But this opening of arms must simply be an invitation. Volf makes a critical distinction at this juncture, claiming that a mutual desire for an act of embrace should exist by both parties. "This is what distinguishes embrace from grasping after the other and holding the other in one's power."[3] If we open our arms to a poor or needy person, we must wait for that person to respond to our gesture. Imposing our will on the other person and forcing that person to reciprocate our gesture, even if our heart is in the right place, does not make for an authentic road-crossing experience.

This idea of *waiting* raises important questions for those of us who want to cross roads toward people—especially to those who are vulnerable and in need. Many Christian ministries talk about "outreach" and "charity." The problem with outreach and charity is that it often keeps people "out of reach," rarely allowing for the potential of a true embrace to exist. We approach the poor, with good intentions and arms that are physically open, in the name of Jesus. But our approach is too often with power and impatience, not with patience and humility. Rather than discovering the deeper story and meeting the human behind the need, we see only the surface situation. We are content with being first-floor Christians. According to Volf, bypassing the waiting period can have detrimental results in the process of creating an authentic road crossing.

ACT THREE: CLOSING OUR ARMS WITH AN EMBRACE

Volf's third act is *closing* the arms. After opening one's arms and waiting, there is a moment when both parties decide to mutually embrace one another. As Volf claims, "It takes two *pairs* of arms for *one* embrace." If only one person in the party wants to embrace, it is still only an invitation. Or if someone clutches for another person, there is no respect.[4] When we close our arms on our enemy, on the neighbor we fear, or on the wayward teen we have mentored, we want to make sure there is reciprocity.

I may not close my arms around the other too tightly, so as to crush her and assimilate her, otherwise I will be engaged in a concealed power-act of exclusion; an embrace would be perverted into a "bear-hug." Similarly, I must keep the boundaries of my own self firm, offer resistance, otherwise I will be engaged in a self-destructive act of abnegation. . . . In an embrace the identity of the self is both preserved and transformed.[5]

This dance between preserving our identity and being receptive to growth is one of the great challenges of road crossing. Young missionaries coming to the inner city from more affluent communities will often work really hard at "fitting in" and denying the unique attributes that have shaped whom they have become. These missionaries from the suburbs try to become "hip" like their urban counterparts—which they are not. This attempt to become something we are not diminishes the opportunity for a true embrace.

When I think of the Christmas Eve scene described in the movie *Joyeux Noël* when enemies came together in the middle of a battlefield and discovered one another's humanness, I am struck by the fact that each group still held on to their ethnic identities. The French remained French; the Germans, German; the British, British; the Scots, Scottish. The scene demonstrates what Volf tries valiantly to communicate. True embrace can take place only if we still maintain our individuality. We do not have to become someone we are not. We can hold on to our identity and yet fully engage with those on the other side of the road and grow from our encounter.

ACT FOUR: LETTING GO

As the final act of embrace, it is critical to understand that we are eventually called to *let go*. Volf contends that we must be able to let go so that our genuine dynamic identity may be preserved. This is the critical difference. When we retreat from the embrace we return "enriched by the traces that the presence of the other has left."[6]

One of the ministry commitments at UrbanPromise is to bring college volunteers and inner-city Camden youth together for meaningful road-crossing experiences. After facilitating these exchanges, we hope that our college volunteers will leave for home or school with a broadened perspective of the world, as will the inner-city students. When our lives take on *traces* of the other—whether thoughts, perspectives, pains, or joys—we become different people with a different outlook on life. We do not lose ourselves, but we enhance ourselves without the desire to overpower or negate the other.

For the college student who visits the inner city, the hope is that these traces of the other will lead to the pursuit of justice for those who are oppressed, help them become more compassionate people, and encourage other-centered career choices. For the inner-city high school student who has grown up in an excluded and poor community, the hope is that the traces of the other will inspire vision to reach beyond their immediate neighborhoods and share their gifts and voice with a bigger world.

If I cross the road to embrace a poor person, my hope is that I will leave the encounter seeing life a little from that person's perspective: some of the unique triumphs and the debilitating injustices he or she faces. If I cross the road to embrace my enemy, my hope is that I leave understanding his or her fragile humanity and deep-rooted insecurities. If I cross the road to embrace someone of another ethnic group, my hope is that I would leave appreciating his or her distinctiveness. If I cross the road to arrive in a place that has been deemed unsafe or populated by "those people," my hope is that my fears are converted into knowledge and insight. In all of these road crossings, I retain my identity and unique story. But with each crossing I return with more pieces of the whole story—the larger human story in which God asks me to participate.

NOTES

Introduction

1. UrbanPromise Ministries is a 501(c)(3) nonprofit that seeks to equip inner-city children and teens with the skills necessary for academic achievement, life management, spiritual growth, and Christian leadership. Visit www.urbanpromiseusa.org for more information.

Chapter One

1. Rodney Clapp, "Signs and Wonderings," *Prism* 7, no. 5 (September/October 2000): 6.
2. Ibid.

Chapter Two

1. Albert Camus, *Notebooks 1935–1942*, trans. Philip Thody (New York: Alfred A. Knopf, 1963), 13–14.
2. Ronald Marstin, *Beyond Our Tribal Gods: The Maturing of Faith* (Maryknoll, NY: Orbis Books, 1979), 3.

Chapter Three

1. Nicholas Wolterstorff, *Lament for a Son* (Grand Rapids: Eerdmans, 1987), 86.
2. An Interview with Nicholas Wolterstorff, "Rights and Wrongs," *Christian Century* (25 March 2008): 28.
3. Ibid., emphasis added.
4. Ibid., 28.

Chapter Four

1. David Gonzalez, "Bronx Priest Fights for Jamaica's Poor," *New York Times* (22 November 2001).
2. Alan Levin, "Plan to Reroute NYC Air Traffic Challenged," *USA Today*, 12 August 2008). Levin writes, "Some of the nation's wealthiest neighborhoods are mounting a fierce legal challenge to block a government plan to untangle air traffic." In wealthy neighborhoods, things like changing airplane routes are challenged in court, because they negatively impact a neighborhood. In poor communities people are often voiceless.
3. Ronald Marstin, *Beyond Our Tribal Gods: The Maturing of Faith* (Maryknoll, NY: Orbis Books, 1979), 128–129.
4. Ibid., 58.

Chapter Five

1. Judith Gundry-Volf, "Spirit, Mercy, and the Other," *Theology Today* 51, no. 4 (1995): 510.
2. Brenda Salter McNeil, "A More Excellent Way: Race & Gender Reconciliation through Christ," *Prism* 7, no. 3 (May/June 2000).
3. Gundry-Volf, "Spirit, Mercy, and the Other," 511.
4. Ibid., 513.
5. Laurent A. Parks Daloz, Cheryl H. Keen, James P. Keen, and Sharon Daloz Parks, *Common Fire* (Boston: Beacon Press, 1996), 63.
6. Ibid., 77.
7. Ibid., 67.
8. Mary Watkins, "In Dreams Begin Responsibilities: Moral Imagination and Action," (paper delivered at the conference Facing Apocalypse, Salve Regina College, Newport, RI, June 1983).
9. Cornel West, *Race Matters* (Boston: Beacon Press, 2001), 42.
10. Daloz, *Common Fire*, 77.

Chapter Six

1. This quote is often attributed to the Protestant reformer, Martin Luther.
2. See George Barna's article, "Changing Church to Save the Gospel," *Prism* (September/ October 2000), where he argues that young people are leaving our churches to find their spiritual nurture in Internet chat rooms. Why? Because there they can be honest and not be judged.
3. M. Scott Peck, *The Different Drum* (New York: Simon and Schuster, 1987), 88.

Chapter Seven

1. Tony Hendra, *Father Joe* (New York: Random House, 2004), 118.
2. Søren Kierkegaard, *Provocations*, ed. Charles E. Moore (Farmington, PA: Plough Publishing House, 2002), 201.
3. Richard John Neuhaus, *Death on a Friday Afternoon* (New York: Basic Books, 2000), 1.
4. Henri Nouwen, *Letters to Marc about Jesus* (San Francisco: HarperSanFrancisco, 1988), 59–61.

Chapter Eight

1. Dorothy Wickenden, "Going Positive," *The New Yorker* (5 May 2008): 23–24.
2. Michael Oreskes, "Lee Atwater, Master of Tactics for Bush and GOP, Dies at 40," *New York Times*, 30 March 1991.
3. Wickenden, "Going Positive," 24.
4. Ibid.

Chapter Nine

1. Joseph S. Nye Jr., *The Powers to Lead* (New York: Oxford University Press, 2008), 13.

Chapter Ten

1. Elie Wiesel, "The Perils of Indifference," the White House, Millennium Lecture, April 12, 1999, www.americanrhetoric.com/speeches/ewieselperilsofindifference.html.
2. Elie Wiesel, "One Must Not Forget (The Evil of Indifference to Tragedy)," *U.S. News & World Report* (27 October 1986): 68.
3. Wiesel, "The Perils of Indifference."

4. Samuel P. Oliner and Pearl M. Oliner, *The Altruistic Personality* (New York: The Free Press, 1988), 174.
5. Thomas Merton, quoted in John Moffit, ed., "Marxism and Monastic Perspectives," *A New Charter for Monasticism* (Notre Dame, IN: University of Notre Dame Press, 1970), 80.

Chapter Twelve

1. Paul Tournier, *A Listening Ear* (Minneapolis: Augsburg, 1987), 19.
2. Mark Oppenheimer, "Miroslav Volf Spans Conflicting Worlds," *Christian Century* (11 January 2003): 18–23.
3. Miroslav Volf, *Exclusion and Embrace* (Nashville: Abingdon Press, 1996), 141.
4. Ibid., 141–145. For a more detailed account of Volf's four stages of embrace, please see Appendix B.
5. Oppenheimer, "Miroslav Volf Spans Conflicting Worlds."

Chapter Thirteen

1. Jason Byassee, "Gangs and God," *Christian Century* (18 September 2007): 20.
2. Ibid.
3. Richard Rohr with John Feister, *Jesus' Plan for a New World* (Cincinnati: St. Anthony Messenger Press, 1996), 144.
4. Visit www.UrbanTrekkers.org to learn about this incredible ministry.

Conclusion

1. William Sloane Coffin, *Credo* (Louisville: Westminster John Knox Press, 2004), 72.

Appendix B

1. Miroslav Volf, *Exclusion and Embrace* (Nashville: Abingdon Press, 1996), 141.
2. Ibid., 69.
3. Ibid., 143.
4. Ibid.
5. Ibid.
6. Ibid., 145.

ABOUT THE AUTHOR

Bruce D. Main invests in young people. In 1988 he founded UrbanPromise Ministries in Camden, New Jersey, to help inner-city youth succeed in all aspects of life through the Christian-based programs offered. Under his leadership, the ministry provides after-school programs, summer camps, employment-readiness programs, entrepreneurial-training opportunities, missionary internships, alternative schools for teens, and the CamdenForward School—an alternative grade-school experience for children from low-income families. In 1997, the vision expanded to include comprehensive youth programs in Canada, Malawi, and Honduras under UrbanPromise Ministries International.

Selected by *Christianity Today* magazine as one of America's "Up-and-Coming Leaders under 40," Bruce Main received a BA in theology from Azusa Pacific University, an MA in theology from Fuller Theological Seminary, and a DMin from Princeton Theological Seminary. He has taught as an adjunct faculty member at Eastern University, Princeton Seminary, and Fuller Theological Seminary, and has been a featured speaker at mission conferences, colleges, and churches. Bruce contributed to *Revolution & Renewal: How Churches Are Saving Our Cities* by Dr. Tony Campolo. His recent books include *Spotting the Sacred: Noticing God in the Most Unlikely Places* and *Holy Hunches: Responding to the Promptings of God*. He and his wife, Pamela, and their three children live in New Jersey. For more information on UrbanPromise Ministries, visit www.urbanpromiseusa.org.

A spiritual jolt for when your respectable faith becomes deadly dull

HOLY FOOLS

Following Jesus with Reckless Abandon

M A T H E W   W O O D L E Y

Why settle for complacency when God offers us so much more?

Mathew Woodley's groundbreaking debut book introduces us to the holy fools (from the desert fathers to Christ himself) who were gutsy enough to push against the grain of society, even to the point of appearing extreme and foolish. Yet God used them to ignite the church to follow Jesus and bring his love to the margins of society—and he can use you in the same way. Ancient and fresh, self-deprecating and honest, *Holy Fools* will shake up your spiritual life and inspire you to pursue a faith without limits.

"A moving and humble book. . . [Woodley's] recasting of Christian dedication as holy folly is appealingly new."—*Library Journal*

"This is the real deal. It challenged me and made me want to grow up."
—Kevin Miller, executive vice president, Christianity Today International

"A literary feast."—Leonard Sweet, professor, Drew Theological School and George Fox University

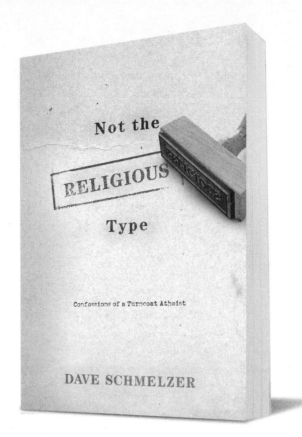

Not the

RELIGIOUS

Type

Confessions of a Turncoat Atheist

DAVE SCHMELZER

In the tradition of C. S. Lewis's *Mere Christianity* and G. K. Chesterton's *Orthodoxy* comes this illuminating collection of thoughts on faith in a postmodern world, one that will help both secularists who never imagined they would become people of faith and also people of faith who perhaps haven't experienced all from God that they've hoped.

"With prose as warm and conversational as an old friend just trying to share some good news, former atheist Dave Schmelzer does an admirable job here of encouraging us to look at the possibility of a life rooted in the mystical, a life where a faith in Jesus is not restrictive but freeing. As someone who could well be called an unbeliever, I find this book to shine with the kind of non-judgment that might, just might, get me to consider much of what Dave Schmelzer gracefully argues here."
—Andre Dubus III, author of *House of Sand and Fog*

"In the combined clarity and sophistication of his message, Dave Schmelzer has become very much an American C. S. Lewis."
—Gregory Crane, professor of classics, Tufts University

CP0380